Envision YOU: UnStuck and C[...]
Kathy Burrus has developed a t[...]
of your life and develop a path [...]
lasting confidence. This powerful [...]
remarkable story you were designed to live.

Tamela Pitts, Writer
tamelapitts.com

Envision YOU *is a gracious invitation to take an honest look at you and*
your life so you can confidently embrace your true self.

Danielle Bernock
Author of *Emerging With Wings*
daniellebernock.com

We may not always feel like the beautiful creations we are, but inward
beauty and the do-it-afraid kind of courage is what really shines. We
can stop striving to be the perfect wife, mother, daughter, friend, leader.
We can just be, because God calls us to rest in Him. When we do, we
melt into who we really are—and we can be real with God. **EnVision**
YOU *will help us notice as God invites us to see Him and step into who*
we really are.

Doris Swift
Author of *Goodbye, Regret*
dorisswift.com

EnVision YOU *is a must read for anyone struggling through the journey*
of grief. (I've read some chapters multiple times because they were so
uplifting). It helped me get unstuck in my grief by allowing me to realize
that I had more to grieve than just my daughter's death. I was able to
accept the fact that I was responsible for my own personal journey and
that God was with me all the way, even before the journey started.

Deb Gyetvai, Registered Nurse

An enlightening book, **EnVision YOU** *is packed with strength and*
wisdom grounded in God's word. A light dawned for me when the
author described the Red Sea experience. A thoughtful way to navigate
crisis and grow in our lives.

Laura McCoy, Author

EnVision YOU *is not just a book. It's a conversation. It's like a cozy chat with a dear friend. You can kick your shoes off and be comfortable. At the same time, you will roll up your sleeves and get to work. Kathy's tender compassion shines through these pages, yet she cares enough to ask us to dig down deep and answer the hard questions that will move us forward on our journey of becoming more and more of who we truly are. Grab a friend and take this next step. No more excuses!*

Lori T. Pruett
Education and Communication Coach

I met Kathy in person and immediately read her first book Lovely Traces of Hope. *Kathy's interaction and honesty with her daughter's story caused me to process my own grief after the loss of a brother and mom one year apart. I was stuck. In Kathy's new book,* **EnVision YOU: UnStuck and Confident,** *you will learn from someone who knows about being stuck and walks you through a process to move forward in confidence and clarity.*

Hazel Dahl Behrens, Retired pastor with new mission
to provide tools and hope for friends walking
beside those facing the bear of mental illness.
about.me/hazel.dahlbehrens

Kathy Burrus gives us real life examples that resonate deeply. **EnVision YOU** *provides practical tools using the acronym SHAPE: Spiritual gifts, Heart, Abilities, Personality, Experiences. You'll not only get unstuck, but you'll appreciate your God-given emotions, and gain confidence with practical application and wisdom toward your authentic self.*

Judy Herman, LPC-MHSP
Author of *Beyond Messy Relationships:
Divine Invitations To Your Authentic Self*
judycounselor.com/beyond-messy-relationships/

EnVision YOU: UnStuck and Confident *is a life-giving resource for anyone that is experiencing a season of self-doubt or "blurred vision". Kathy Burrus shares her hard-won wisdom so generously, including a free workbook to ensure a personalized, actionable process. What are you waiting for?*

Kathy Rushing, MS, LPC
Host of the podcast, *Committed: The Entrepreneur Marriage*
kathyrushing.com

One of the benefits of reading **EnVision YOU** *is to help you see clearly who God made you to be and to help you to overcome places where Satan and your own sin or the sin of others has caused you to become stuck. This book will help you discover ways of finding freedom and joy.*

Lydia Tschetter
Pastor's Wife, Leader of Women

*Honest, open, raw, vulnerable—***EnVision YOU** *gracefully invites and challenges us to identify and confront our stuck places, as only then can we imagine, dream and emerge the confident and courageous beings we were designed to be.*

Sue P. Nash, PhD

EnVision YOU *found me in the middle of my fifth year of severe burnout. Within the first pages I was in tears—hope?! Hope was something for other people—those who have choices left in life. Yet as I read through these pages, I discovered a tender seed planted in my heart . . . maybe, just maybe, there could be hope for me too. I love the honesty of Kathy's writing and the exercises included to move these concepts from "nice to read" to "in my heart." Although my circumstances have not changed, I can say ***EnVision You** *has returned the impossible— hope—to my life again.*

Cheryl Sherwin

*Being stuck is hard. Getting unstuck is hard too. Kathy knows that because she's been there, and she lovingly walks you through the process. I've been fortunate enough to work through my stuck places at Kathy's kitchen table, with her guiding me. That is the best way to do it, but you'll get pretty close if you read ***EnVision YOU.** *You will hear her voice and her uncanny way of having just the right question come out almost as if she's right there with you.*

Lean into the process. It will be hard. But it will be worth it. You can trust Kathy. She'll help you see your Savior and hear what he is telling you about yourself and your circumstances. You'll find yourself stepping into a new confidence you never thought you would have.

Beth Moore
copywriter and content strategist
bmooreconnected.com

I loved **EnVision You: Unstuck and Confident***! This book embodies the things that I talk about in my business: being confident and authentic to who you are. Kathy explains why you aren't ordinary and has a life map to walk you through your story! Kathy has been through a lot (like the death of a child), yet still, she fights for confidence and is pushing herself to be unstuck. She is the true picture of a warrior. Her message of getting unstuck and pursuing the life you want resonated with me! My favorite part is that there is a workbook to walk you through it and make the process actionable!*

Marie Sonneman
OrdinarytoBadass.com

You are unique and powerful. You have everything you need to succeed, but if God is nudging you to reach out for help, it may be time to take the next step. **EnVision YOU** *will help you find your voice and your words that have the power to change your life and the lives of others. They deserve to be set free and make a difference in the world.*
EnVision YOU: UnStuck and Confident!

Deanne Welsh
Writing Coach and Copy Editor
deannewelsh.com

ENVISION YOU

Dear Hannah
& Jennifer (Santos)

I wrote this book for
women like you who know God
made them for a special Purpose!
I hope those words will inspire you
to continue your journey to make
your remarkable difference in
the world.

You matter!
your message matters!

Kathy Burns
Sept 22

ENVISION YOU

UNSTUCK AND CONFIDENT

EMBRACE YOUR TRUTH
AND MAKE YOUR REMARKABLE DIFFERENCE

KATHY BURRUS

Cover designer: Rob Williams, Fiverr.com/cal5086

Author Photography: Brandon Hendrix and Rosebelle Easthom,
    BrandonandRosePhotography.com

Editor & Creative Team:

Kim Carr, On The Mark Editorial Services, kimsonthemark.com
Beth Moore, BMoore | Connected, bmooreconnected.com
Brielle Augsburger

To the women
who have inspired me to live unstuck
and see myself, my world, and my God
in new and different ways
since the day they were born.

My beautiful daughters,
Caitlin, Brielle, and Leisha

—⁓—

To the women in my life
who have dared to rise to the challenge
of being all they are made to be,
of doing the hard work of becoming unstuck,
of taking bold next steps
with a confidence that comes from their Creator.

Here's to the difference each of you make
in my life and your world!

Download your free 45-page workbook

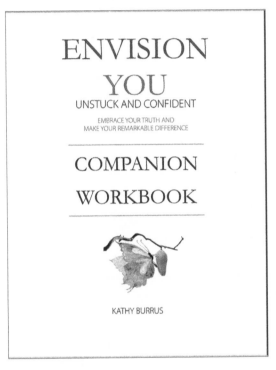

ENVISION
YOU
UNSTUCK AND CONFIDENT

EMBRACE YOUR TRUTH AND
MAKE YOUR REMARKABLE DIFFERENCE

COMPANION

WORKBOOK

KATHY BURRUS

to help you capture and process the insights and awarenesses you have as you read through the material.

To download, go to
kathyburrus.com/envision-you-workbook.

CONTENTS

FOREWORD

EnVision YOU by Kathy Burrus is a book for anyone who longs to make a difference, embrace their purpose and do things that matter.

- If your way is murky and you are unsure of what the next step should be, this book is for you.

- If you have a passion to make an impact in the lives around you, but you lack the confidence to step out into new territory, this book is for you.

- If you have more questions about God's desire for you than answers, this book is for you.

Kathy is a precious soul who understands where you are, because just a little bit ago she was there too. The words she shares so passionately are practical, soul searching and even funny at times. She is a woman who leads with gentle empathy and hope, all while being courageous enough to push you just enough (trust me you won't hardly know she is pushing) to think a little or a lot differently about the moments you have been given in this life. She believes passionately in your innate ability to grow, reach and become more of who God has created and called you to be.

This book holds unforgettable truths on purpose, value, confidence and trying again all woven into doable real-life steps which have the potential to change your way of thinking. It is a book for the woman who wants to quit but is afraid of what it will cost her deep inside and who she would become if she did.

This book is for the woman who is ready try again, dust off, stand up and take a breath, all while repeating in a whisper,

not giving up.

not ever.

not giving up today or tomorrow either.

not giving up.

If you are looking to get unstuck and move from where you are to where you sense God is calling you to be, I invite you in to explore what it means to Envision a new way of living and being.

Ready for change? Start with the first page . . . and read one glorious word at a time. I promise, you won't be able to put it down.

Nancy Bouwens is a certified coach for women who are navigating mid-life. Her incredible passion and joy is encouraging them to live life on purpose, be present and believe nothing is impossible, so they can live a life without regret, discover joy and impact their corner of world in ways they never thought possible.

Her motto is "Live the Story You Want Your Life to Tell." If you would like to connect with Nancy, find her by email: hello@ nancybouwens.com or at her blog, "The Intentional Life."

This Book is For YOU!

HELLO, MY FRIEND,

You must be a woman who believes you were made to make a difference in your world. You want to do things that matter. You want to leave a legacy that helps to address a need you see or a problem people face.

How do I know this about you?

Why would you pick up a book called **EnVision YOU: Unstuck and Confident** unless you are trying to take some significant next steps but finding you are unable to do so for some reason?

What does it look like to live and work confidently to make a difference in your world? What does it feel like to step into your uniqueness, your beauty that forms the foundation for your confidence?

I imagine it feels something like a butterfly must feel as she spreads her wings for the first time and finds freedom to soar higher than ever before.

Where would you like to take bold next steps with that kind of confidence?

The word *envision* is defined in two parts. *Vision,* as a noun, is *the faculty or state of being able*

1

to see. When it is used as a verb (which is an action word), it means to *imagine!*

Not surprising, *en* is a *prefix* or sometimes a *suffix.* When added to a word at either end, **en changes the other word.** Usually it turns a noun into a verb, or perhaps an adjective that, if you remember, is a descriptive word.

Why is this little English lesson so important?

Well, *en* generally means *to cause a person or thing (which are nouns) to be **in** the place, condition, or state named by the stem word.* Sounds like a pretty cool little word.

When *en* **(to cause to be in)** is partnered with *vision* **(to be able to see; imagine)** this amazing thing happens. . .

We can see the future as if we were dropped into our desired outcome!

All by itself, the definition of *en* doesn't say anything about the future. It just has the ability to *cause to be in.* But when you cause something to be *in vision*, you can imagine or visualize future possibilities.

YOU SEE MORE!

But my guess is that you struggle to accept who you truly are as being enough for more! Before you can *EnVision YOU* at all, you must first break free of the STUCK places that keep you from believing in yourself.

You not only DON'T feel confident, you DO feel stuck.

As a woman who knows that feeling, I have discovered—or I should say rediscovered for the first time—that this process to find our way through STUCK is not a journey of well-organized steps along a straight path. It's more a circle of steps, much like the metamorphosis of the caterpillar to butterfly.

As we work the circle of our own transformation, we, at times, are required to stop simply to pay attention to our lives, to look deep within ourselves, and to take an honest look at what's real about who we are, our circumstances, and our story.

In that deep place, we gain courage and strength to do the hard work of breaking free of the stuck places—the emotions, messages, even grief from our past—in order to move forward.

And then comes that moment where we not only *EnVision* or **see the possibilities** but we step forward into them with boldness and confidence knowing we are where we need to be. We *soar!*

How would that feel?

Why should you listen to me? Good question!

I am a certified professional life coach and a coach of coaches as an instructor at the school where I received my coaching credentials. I have spent my entire adult life working in ministry, walking alongside others as they break free of the STUCK and break through to BE who they were made to be.

But I'm not writing as any guru. **My guess is you really don't care about all that anyway.**

The truth is that I wrote this book because I needed this book. I am a woman who has had to break free of STUCK in order to survive, let alone thrive. I have wrestled with layers of what's real and what's stuck, primarily since losing my 15-year-old daughter in a car/pedestrian accident over a dozen years ago. There have been health issues, job losses, and dreams dying that have been part of my journey as well.

These were overwhelming times in my journey when I couldn't imagine ever being able to walk again, let alone soar with "wind beneath my wings."

I want you to know that I get it. I know what it is like to deal with the hardness of life and yet find hope, joy, and even life again. I have witnessed transformations in other women that continue to inspire me even as I walk the journey with them.

We have been given an invitation to *be*, to break through to who we really are, and to live confident that our lives matter and make a difference in our world. We don't always *feel* confident, but we *know* confidence, if that makes sense.

My heart for you, dear woman who longs to make a difference, is that you will have the courage to work through your layers of stuck and find that place of confidence as you take your best next steps.

How does this book benefit you?

EnVision YOU: Unstuck and Confident provides a clear path to help you break free of the tethers that keep you tied to *stuck*. That means you are going to need to do some work—hard work. Just reading this book won't change anything for you. But the work is essential to *EnVision* the possibilities as you move forward with confidence.

Through this book, you will look at ways to:

- Accept who you really are
- Embrace the significance of your whole story
- Honor your emotions and why you feel the way you do
- Ask the hard questions to figure out where you are stuck and what you grieve
- Pay attention to what you are noticing in and around you
- Choose how you want to respond to what life offers you

This book, along with the free downloadable workbook designed to help you capture your insights, will allow you to see the work you need to do and help you do it.

There is support and accountability built into this journey. I invite you to connect with me and engage with other women much like yourself as if we were sharing notes over a cup of coffee. Hearing the stories of others reminds us we are not alone in the struggle and encourages us as we hear how others succeed.

You may want to jump around in the book. I mean it *is* more fun to explore the possibilities, right? But I encourage you to read all the way through the book to get the big picture first. There will be some chapters that resonate with you more than others. Pay attention to the questions that jump out to you. They connect for a reason.

Even in the process of testing out this material, women have shared how they have broken free from their own stuck places.

> *"I discovered I was stuck in areas that I didn't even realize. Now I can see where and why I'm stuck and can work toward becoming unstuck."*

> *"I realized that it is ok to cry, to feel the way I do about myself."*

> *"I was touched by grieving the death of my daughter but also all the other changes in my life because of that. I now recognize those unwanted changes as part of the loss. Instead of frustration, anger, and guilt about feeling upset, I can grieve the loss I already feel."*

I Promise...

You have that capacity to *EnVision YOU: Unstuck and Confident:*

- To own what's real—the good and the bad of it.
- To embrace what is stuck and find ways to overcome it.
- To pay attention to the ways God invites you to influence.
- To see the possibilities that lay ahead.
- To do what matters most to you.

You, my friend, have what it takes to soar as you make your remarkable difference in the world. You may not see it as remarkable because it is such an ordinary part of who you are and what you do.

But when you do YOU, it makes an extraordinary difference elsewhere.

Before you jump into the book, I invite you to do three things:

1. **Download the free workbook** to help you capture and process the insights and awarenesses you have as you read through the material. Go here to download:

   kathyburrus.com/envision-you-workbook

2. **Invite a girlfriend to be your buddy** and work through this process with you. She can download the Kindle version or order a print copy. Make sure she gets the workbook too.

3. **Join the *EnVision YOU: Unstuck and Confident* Facebook community** to add some additional accountability and support to your journey. I'll be showing up there periodically to talk through some of the topics we discuss in the book. Find out how to join when you download the workbook.

Ok! Pour yourself a cup of your favorite beverage and join me in these pages. The pace you work through this material is up to you and your buddy. So, if you want to skim through the book and then come back to work through the chapters that seem to connect most, that's fine. Just remember, at some point we all start back at the beginning.

PART ONE

WHAT GOT YOUR ATTENTION?

I WROTE THIS book because, first of all, I want you to know you are not alone. But secondly, to remind you that you are, no matter where you are in your journey, **in the perfect place for amazing transformation to come about in your life**. You may not want to hear that because you aren't sure you like where you are. But it is true.

The little caterpillar teaches us much about that place . . .

There she is trudging along on a small branch, working her little legs very hard to get from one place to another. At some point she begins to resemble a 'J' hanging from a branch as she creates a chrysalis. That is when she begins a remarkable transformation called *metamorphosis*.

-> egg -> caterpillar -> chrysalis -> butterfly

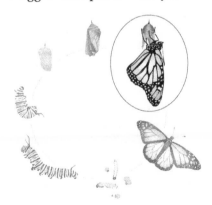

IMAGINE THAT MOMENT —

When the caterpillar

feels the hardness of the

chrysalis give way

She begins to wiggle her way

out—feeling very different

than before

Her very body—though it is weak—feels . . . free, light, full of energy

She is still for a moment—

In awe of the feeling of life surging through her body

Carefully, curiously

she opens her wings

Looking from side to side, she is aware that she has changed a great deal

Though she is not completely aware of her own beauty

We can see her—the vibrant colors, her fragile strength

That suddenly takes wing— wind lifting her higher and higher,
Allowing her to see the world from a completely different perspective

Than when she was crawling

very near to the ground as a caterpillar

Now she soars,

Fluttering from one perch to another

My daughter Leisha with a butterfly that landed on her finger during a hiking trip with her youth group the summer before she died.

You are very much like that little caterpillar. It is only after you choose to do the hard work of going deep within yourself that you can experience the transformation that gives you strength to soar.

You are beginning your journey to discover the *hard* places that teach you who you already are. You will explore how to break free of the *stuck* places and to soar as you were meant to.

Are you ready?

Chapter 1

So, What Changed?

Am I RIGHT to assume that something in your life has changed recently?

It may have to do with your job, a relationship, or even your health. Something has made you stop and pay attention to what is going on in life. I'm guessing, whether you have voiced it yet or not, the question you are asking sounds something like,

Is this all there is?

How do I know? Well, because I've been there too. In fact, as a life coach for women, I talk with clients every day who have come to this same place in life and are asking a very similar question.

Something—it might be marriage, parenting, or a job—isn't what you thought it would be. Or you might have reached a milestone birthday or accomplishment in your life and you are asking questions like "*How did I get here? Is there more to life than what I am doing?*"

Maybe you just woke up one morning to these thoughts. But chances are something in your life changed and *shook you* to this awakening. You are noticing a longing deep inside, a desire that seems to be growing from a core place within you that stirs up memories of a time long ago.

You recall a dream you had of one day growing up and being someone *special,* a difference maker who influenced her world by doing stuff that matters. What that stuff was, you weren't sure, but you wanted to matter in doing it.

However, one of the most common statements I hear from women I work with is . . .

"I want to make a difference in my world, but I'm stuck."

Ever caught yourself saying those words? You want to have a life of significance and influence, but there is this *stuff* going on . . .

- Your spouse walked out of the house after telling you he wasn't happy in your marriage.
- Your child slammed the door in your face after a heated argument.
- Your boss passed you over and gave the promotion to someone younger.
- Your doctor told you some unnerving news about your health.
- You attended a funeral of a long-time friend who died from cancer.
- You had a milestone birthday.

What was the change that made you wake up to the reality that you are stuck and caused you to ask . . .

- *Is this all there is?*
- *Is this how my life is supposed to be?*
- *Does what I do matter to anyone?*
- *Do I matter?*

What was it that caused you to stop and ask if there is more to life?

In my story, several instances *stopped* me over a short span of three years:

- Our family went through some issues that threatened to divide us all.

   We *stopped* how we were doing family and started an intense season of family, marriage, and individual counseling.

- I experienced a health crisis that nearly took my life.

  I *stopped* physically until we found a doctor that knew what was happening in my body. Within hours of the diagnosis of Addison's disease (a disorder in which the adrenal glands stop producing the hormones a body needs) and the first dose of medication, I began to feel life surging through my body again.

- I stepped away from a job I spent all my life preparing for.

  I *stopped* my job for the sake of my health and family. It was hard to walk away from a position I loved, but I couldn't maintain the intensity I had been working.

- My husband walked away from a career we thought would be our lifetime work and we became entrepreneurs.

  We *stopped* the only life we knew and threw ourselves into learning to live and work differently.

Each one of those occurrences 'shook' me and forced me to stop and ask . . .

- *Is this all there is?*
- *What do I do now?*
- *Who am I when I am not in the role I thought I would always play?*

And with each instance there was a new question that had to be answered from a fresh perspective. As I wrestled to find my answers, I found a way to get unstuck and move forward with honest awareness and greater confidence in who I am and what I was made to do.

UNTIL . . .

One year after we changed the course of our careers, our youngest daughter died in a car/pedestrian accident a mile and a half from our home.

"*Shook*" does not begin to describe that moment. I felt as if I were shattered into a million pieces. Parts of me felt dead, but the rest of me was alive enough to feel the excruciating pain over and over again.

The purpose of this book is not to dwell on my story. I'll refer to it throughout these pages, but you can read the whole story in my first book, Lovely Traces of Hope[1]. *See resource page in workbook for details.*

At this point, I wasn't asking *"Is this all there is?"*

I was screaming: *"How can I ever survive this pain for the rest of my life? How can I ever LIVE again after being broken—DEAD—inside?"*

Why do I share all of this with you?

Because you need to know that I *know.*
I get it.
I get you.
You are not alone.
I'm not going to shame you for where you are.
I've been there.
I know how ugly life can be.

But I'm also here to tell you *there is hope!*

I never dreamed I would feel HOPE—or LIFE—strongly again, but I do. And I have walked with many women who have come to a new awareness of who they are and what they are meant to do with their lives. You will hear some of their stories in the pages to come.

They join me in speaking truth that there is

- A gift in being SHOOK to the point of stopping.
- LIFE after death or traumatic events.
- HOPE!

You can choose to ignore the HARD and STUCK places, keep busy to avoid feeling the pain, or find ways to distract yourself from the fact that it really hurts. But most likely, you will be forced to reckon with this ache at some point.

What if you embrace it, whatever *it* is, and intentionally choose to grab on to the reality of this moment? See what it shows you about *you* and the remarkable difference you make in your world.

Practice standing with arms stretched wide over your head and with a joyful expression on your face, yell out these words: "*This is how it feels to be* ***me***."

What would it feel like to ***envision yourself unstuck and confident*** as you LIVE the rest of your life?

Let's be transformed together.

I encourage you to:

- **Buddy Check-In: Connect with a girlfriend you trust to join you in the journey.** Share with each other what you hope to accomplish as you work through this book.

- **Download the workbook** if you haven't already. LINK You will notice a section marked "Commitment to Myself." This is your reminder that you have said yes to investing in yourself as you work through this process.

- **Find a space where you feel safe** enough to explore what is *real*. You may choose the same place every day, or a space that changes every day. The key word here is *safe*—a place that allows you to explore, create, and enjoy the moment.

Chapter 2

Why Did You Stop?

I WISH WE could share a cup of tea as we compare stories. I'm sure we would find we have much in common. We have spent a great deal of our lives trying to do things that matter, yet every time we try to take a step forward, we end up struggling with a new stuck place. Or maybe it is an old stuck place that we thought we had dealt with but realize now it has crept back into our lives as a new layer that needs to be reckoned with.

Each time we hit that wall, or ceiling, or whatever our *stuck* looks like today, we begin to question our direction and doubt our skills or ability to get past it. We get bogged down to the point of wanting to quit doing whatever we are doing and become consumed in the HARD STUFF and the STUCK PLACES.

Have you ever felt that way? Like every time you take a step forward you find yourself dealing with yet another place of STUCK?

I really thought that if I was doing what I was supposed to be doing, I wouldn't have to worry about being stuck. Because I hoped I would be sure enough of myself that I wouldn't get bogged down in the unimportant. I would be able to focus all my attention on the HARD parts of success rather than the stuck places that kept me from getting there.

The reality is that every woman preparing to take a new step becomes aware that while she wants to be doing the things that matter to her, there is a season of feeling stuck. It may simply be related to the uncertainty of doing a new thing, or wondering if she has what it takes to do the task ahead.

My story is no different.

The first time I met Jenn Wenzke was at the first meeting of a brand new networking group for women in business. Smiling and friendly, Jenn walked in with a cane, careful not to get caught in the clusters of women and seated herself at the far end of the room. A team of women checked on her often and made sure she had what she needed. You see, Jenn had been diagnosed with ALS (Lou Gehrig's disease) some months earlier and was experiencing the decline in mobility that came with the disease.

I immediately connected with the mission and the spirit of the group—and more specifically with this woman who was here despite her circumstances. Perhaps she was here more *because* of her circumstances, not just her illness but the stories of her life that had threatened to destroy her and any hope of a future she might have.

She had overcome. She was persevering. She was making a difference. I wanted to know her!

As the evening came to a close, I slid into the chair closest to her and listened in as she finished up another conversation. Then she turned to me. She asked for my name and we discussed what we had in common—Mary Kay cosmetics and coaching. She had been a director and driven the awarded MK car for several years, but she had given the car back to pursue life coaching because she desired to speak more deeply into the lives of women. I had only dreamed of the car. I had hit far too many personal ceilings to pursue it further and eventually stepped out of Mary Kay to pursue coaching.

She asked, *"Kathy, do you know your value?"*

I hesitated to reply. I wanted to boldly proclaim, *"Yes, ma'am! I do!"* But the honest truth was, I didn't. I was struggling to know if I really did have something to contribute.

Before I responded, she went on. *"Kathy, do you offer value to your clients?"*

Hmm. . . By then I had been open for business as a life coach for four years. I believed I did offer value to my clients. I was more convinced at that moment than I had been when I started. But it was hard to feel like I had something to offer when I still felt such brokenness from my daughter's death over eight years ago.

Slowly but surely, I was becoming more aware of what I could offer to each woman who coached with me. Not just because I could coach her but because I understood her. I *was* her. Been there! Done that! Still there in some ways!

Then Jenn had one last question: *"Are you charging what you are worth?"*

Uh, no! I knew that answer.

"People really don't understand the value of a coach. People aren't aware of what it is worth to have a coach that helps to move them forward. I just don't think I could really charge what I'm worth for my clients."

"Well," she said, **"when you are done making excuses, you can get on with your business."**

AH! There it is!

In three questions, Jenn had summed up the greatest limiting beliefs of my life. My struggles with these ceilings were revealing a significant erosion of confidence that kept me from being my best self.

I didn't know my own value or the value I offered to others.

The wrestling I was going through to answer the first two questions kept me from being confident enough to answer the third in the affirmative "Yes! I am worth being paid for what I do!"

Yep! That just about said it all. Jenn had me pegged—and we had known each other less than an hour.

What is my value?

Answering that question will probably be an ongoing exercise for the rest of my life. As it might be for you as well. **How would you answer that question?**

I became increasingly aware of this mental game I played with myself. I didn't answer the questions *"Who am I?"* or *"Do I think I have value?"*

Instead, my question sounded more like *"What should I be doing to be who I think I should become?"* So many "should"s in one question. Do you have a question like that in your brain?

I found I wasn't looking for the real me, but for who I thought someone else thought I should be.

And truly, when Jenn asked me if I had value, my thought was more about whether I thought *she* thought what I did had value. Do you see how confusing it can be?

But Jenn never let me get away with that. In my ongoing conversations with Jenn, more than once she inspired me to answer a question similar to this. And more than once reminded me, *"When you are done making excuses, you can get on with your business."*

We'll get to the excuses later on in the book. But that conversation is actually what inspired the book you hold in your hands now. That's where I got the title *EnVision YOU: Unstuck and Confident.*

As I started writing this book, I wanted to focus on the **confidence and the value we offer** to our world—the part of us that has the sparkle and the productivity. I wanted to help women soar with confidence, and I mean SOAR in big, bold ways.

But what I found is that most often women need something else first. The greatest value I offer to women has more to do with the places and spaces **where we are not soaring,** where we feel stuck. After all, we get to a place of soaring only *after* a season of laboring, a time of pushing through hard places and experiencing growing pains.

With an unanswered question as important as knowing my value, I needed to take some time to pay attention to why I couldn't confidently respond.

My conversation with Jenn caused me to STOP to find some answers.

What made you stop?

Were you *forced* to stop by some traumatic or life-altering experience in your life? (Like I was with my health, or family crisis, or the death of our daughter I mentioned earlier.)

Or did you intentionally choose to STOP because you sensed you needed to take a longer look at where you are right now?

Why you stop makes a difference in how you respond to the stopping.

When you are *forced* to stop, your search for answers is often out of desperation. You might end up wrestling with resentment or anger. You might discover that you are resistant to what you must face in the mess of it all. When we are forced to come to a halt, it's often not pretty. We don't like it. We resist it at every turn. It doesn't mean the stopping doesn't have value, but we are in a battle to find that value.

If you *proactively, intentionally* stop in order to step back and look at the big picture of your life *(much like our friend the caterpillar when she enters the chrysalis)*, then your perspective is often more purposeful and productive. You ask questions like *"Is this all there is?"* but with added determination to seek for answers that will lead you to MORE for your life.

There are times when we simply feel the need to stop. Taking that step is a welcome relief. We find rest by discontinuing whatever our activity is.

But we also find it uncomfortable because we work hard to be productive. When we retreat from activities we feel are essential to being productive, we feel unproductive, which prevents us from taking the very steps we need to take to move forward in life or relationships.

WHAT IF the STOPPING is actually an invitation? A personal invitation to notice that God—the God of the universe—is breaking into our world to connect with us.

I don't know what you think about God. I don't know what kind of relationship you might have with him. Or if you believe there is even an opportunity to have a personal relationship with the Divine.

But what if God really is touching your life in this moment?

God, our Creator, designed us with unique strengths and abilities to do what others cannot. He uses our emotions, particularly the intense, feel-it-to-the-core-of-who-you-are kinds of emotions, to get our attention. Our emotions serve as a tap on the shoulder—or sometimes a slap across the face—to say *"Wake up! Do you see what's going on here?"*

Any time you sense an emotion as simple as goosebumps when you hear an incredible story, or sweet joy at the sight of your child or grandchild, you are being invited to notice.

Any time you feel rage well up within you because of an injustice, or excitement at accomplishing a huge goal, you are being invited to pay attention to something God wants to say to you.

How would you describe the moments that stir up your emotions?

Or another question I would ask is *how do you feel about stopping?*

Often I hear women say, *"I need to just keep moving forward. I'm tired of my past. I've dealt with it all I'm going to. Let's just move on."*

It would be great if it were that easy. But these moments from our past—painful or otherwise—tug at our hearts for a reason. While we may have been fervent in our efforts to reckon past relationships or hurts, some new step that we take may, in fact, stir up another layer of reckoning that needs to be done.

We might find that discouraging, as if we didn't do a good job of working through it in the past. But consider if a small child comes to you to learn how to tie their shoes. You work hard to teach them and are proud of all they can do when you finish your lesson. Will you scold them when they come back to you uncertain how to tie a different pair of shoes? Chances are you would realize you need to teach them a new skill to take this next step.

That is true for us as adults as well. We can learn a great deal about ourselves by digging through our past and uncovering the lessons there. But when we take another step in a new direction, it is quite possible that the same something from the past will show up again. We will need to find a new way to "tie up" the past with our present and future circumstances.

How are you managing this interruption to your life?

Stopping can feel like an interruption.

Do you welcome the interruption? Do you embrace the moment to stop as a time to go deeper, to learn more about yourself? Or do you fight it—trying to force action or positive moments, when it seems you simply must move forward?

Stopping can feel counterproductive.

Some comments I've heard from my clients are:

- *Feels like I'm wasting time.*
- *I don't know what to do when I stop.*
- *It is such a challenge to dissect the moments.*
- *I'm a little afraid to be still because of what I might see, feel, or hear.*

We will talk about some of these concepts throughout the book, but for now, the important thing is to identify what you are feeling.

What do you fear most in stopping?

Go ahead and identify it as best you can. Spelling out what makes us afraid will allow us to find ways to work through the fear. We can find tangible ways to overcome an emotion that is causing us to be stuck.

Head over to the workbook and jot down a few sentences that might describe what you feel when you must stop.

Before we move on, consider the definition of STOP:

- to cease from doing
- to cause something to halt
- to come to an end

Which definition best describes WHY you stopped?

- Was it to stop doing something?
- Or make something else stop happening?
- Or to bring something to an end, to finish it?

I really want you to ponder your answer. In fact, I encourage you to write your answer in your workbook. **Why did you stop?**

BUDDY CHECK-IN:

This might be an insightful conversation to have with your accountability buddy. (You did get one, right?) Your girlfriend—and the conversations you can have in a safe space—is an important part of the journey. Consider joining us in the Facebook group to process your awarenesses as you walk through this material.

Chapter 3

Your BIG Longing

WHEN YOU HEAR a friend say *"I want to make a difference, but I feel stuck. I want to feel confident,"* what is your response?

I shout, *"Me too! I want to make a difference too. I want to feel confident too!"*

It happened so often that I began to ask myself:

- Why is this important to me? To women?
- Why do I struggle with wanting to make my difference and feel confident?
- Why do I shut down when I hear the words or anything that resembles a theme like *"not good enough"*?

When I traced my *confidence* story through my past, I landed on a memory of a little 8-year-old girl bubbling over with excitement, blonde curls bouncing, eyes sparkling.

~ ⚬ ~

I wait as patiently as a second grader can for my turn to talk to my teacher. If I were a color, it would be yellow because I am radiating sunshine. I have something wonderful to tell "Mrs. J."

I just found out that the choir songs my class has been practicing are part of a much bigger program that includes special solo parts too. A fourth-grade girl sings the song I especially love. She gets to sing and twirl around with her hands up in the air. I am a quick study of music, and I learn her part very easily, even when to twirl.

As soon as practice is over, I make a beeline to the front of my teacher's desk. I can't wait to tell her that I have already learned that song and can do it really, really well. I am confident once she sees me do it, she will let me do that song for the program.

But for some reason, she doesn't.

Every recess, every lunch hour, any bit of a moment she is alone, I perform my little routine for her, always asking if I can do that part. Each time, she graciously listens to my song and compliments my dance.

"Yes, you do that very well, but that part belongs to the fourth grader already."

"Honey, you can't do that part, somebody else is already doing it."

"Kathy, somebody else is doing it this year. When you are a fourth grader, you can do a special part too."

But on one particular day, after she listens to my pleas for yet a thousandth time, Mrs. J turns her wooden swivel chair toward me, puts her hands gently on my shoulders, and says,

"Kathy, honey, you're just not good enough."

I gasp!

Oh! That's a different story. I was confident that if I showed her how well I could do it and gave the best of everything I had, it would be good. But if after all of that,

Mrs. J says it's not good enough, well, all my second-grade heart could understand is that *I* must not be good enough.

As I got on the bus the morning of the spring musicale wearing my cute little pink Easter dress, I threw up all over Sol, the bus driver. All I could think was *what if I'm not good enough to be in the chorus either?*

Why did I tell you that story?

Because when I stopped to consider the VALUE question Jenn had asked me, I recalled this little story. I realized all the times I asked, Mrs. J must have said something like *"Yes, Kathy, you do that very well, but the older kids were assigned the parts. Maybe next year you can do one of them."*

But that didn't stop me. I kept pursuing—with the confidence of a second grader—because I just *knew* I could do it.

Until I heard the words *"you're just not good enough!"* For some reason, I heard those words. I accepted those words. I threw up my hands and walked away.

Inside my heart, a piece of my confidence was stripped away, and one more belief was laid bare that I cannot be confident that who I am and what I was made to do was good enough.

What kind of AHAs do you have when you STOP and take time to notice?

This might be an insightful conversation to have with your girlfriend that you invited on the journey in Chapter 1. Accountability is an important part of the process.

No matter what caused you to stop, the opportunity you have now is significant. This is the time to **notice what you are noticing!**

What is coming up in your heart, your thoughts, and your spirit?

I believe that God is our Creator. He designed you and me in some very special ways. Not only did he shape our bodies and our faces to resemble our parents, but he gave us skills, abilities, and talents, which we may or may not have developed yet. He designed our personalities and passions to do special things that others aren't made to do. And he planted within the core of our being a dream that is designed for us.

Could it be that there is a longing bubbling up in you? You may think it is a desire for something *more*, something bigger or better that you want in your life.

But perhaps it has always been there. You sense that you were made for something special. But it is not until you come to a stop that you have the opportunity to become more aware of it.

Let's call it the *big longing **to make a difference in your world.*** You may not always use those words. It might come out more like, I want to . . .

- Make a difference.
- Do stuff that matters.
- Have a purpose.
- Want what God wants for me.
- Feel confident.
- Be able to influence my world.
- Want more.

Let's take a look at this BIG LONGING by taking time to open your awareness of what you want deep down in your core. It might be something that you thought you wanted to do last New Year's Day when you were making your resolutions. Or it may be something that was tied to a dream you had in college or even as a small child.

Think about it.

Close your eyes and let your thoughts take you back to a time when you were a child, maybe seven or eight years old. Picture yourself in your room sitting on your bed. Open your mind's eye, and observe what you are seeing around you.

- What color is your room?
- What is hanging on the walls?
- Is your bed made or unmade as if you just crawled out from under the covers?
- What else is in your room? Toys, books, colors or paints, paper . . .

Where in your room do you keep your special treasures? Do you keep them in a pencil box under the bed, or hidden in a paper sack in the back of a drawer?

What are those special things that you keep? Why are they important to you?

What do they tell you about yourself?

Perhaps you were filled with hopes and dreams of being someone important, someone people looked up to and respected.

Maybe you wanted to be just like your mom when you grew up. You wanted to care for your home and family, be a volunteer for community and church events, or perhaps run your own business like she did.

Or maybe you wanted to just feel safe. Your home life wasn't great. All you hoped for was a place where you didn't have to worry about your next meal or what would happen when your parents got home. *(If that is the case, I am sorry. This exercise might be pretty difficult for you. It might be good if you do this exercise with your buddy, but I encourage you to continue as best you can to see what your childhood can teach you about who you are now.)*

What did you think about yourself as a child?

What were the words you said or thought when you imagined yourself as a grown-up? Maybe it was something like "I want to be a doctor, or a nurse, or an astronaut . . ." or maybe it was "I want to be special, important, seen . . ."

What do you remember wanting to be when you grew up?

Jot down some ideas in the workbook.

Now look at those things you have written, and see if you can identify words to describe how you envisioned yourself in that role. For instance, when I was a child, I wanted whatever role I imagined for myself (music teacher, missionary, pastor's wife) to be someone special. I wanted to be someone who made other people feel special. I didn't know at that age why that was important to me, I just knew I wanted to be someone that treated people the way I want to be treated—special.

Whether I knew it or not, even as a small child I was determining how I would behave, how I would treat people, and how I would respond to people and circumstances. If I wanted to be special, I would need to respond in a way that was special.

That may seem like such a simple observation. Why go to all the work of remembering and digging into something we thought as a child? Well, because that underlying longing is still speaking into who we are today. We may not put it all together until we work through it as grown-ups, but many decisions in our lives have been based on our childhood beliefs.

Even my longing to be a life coach and help women just like yourself was born out of that childhood longing to make a difference by being someone special who treated people special.

BUDDY CHECK-IN:

Here are some questions you can ponder and share with your accountability buddy:

- How does what you remember about your longings as a child tie into this BIG LONGING you notice in your life now?

- What are some ways you notice your childhood longing affecting your behaviors and decisions even today?

- Is your BIG LONGING worth working through the HARD stuff for?

On a scale of 1-10 (10 being very committed) how committed are you to do the HARD stuff ahead of you? Remember, you are doing this in order to break free of the stuck places. Then you can break through to accomplish that BIG LONGING in your heart.

Find a safe space where you will be free to explore what is really in your heart.

Remember, I invited you to make a commitment with yourself—and your buddy—that you will finish what you have started even when it gets hard.

Isn't your BIG LONGING worth it?

Chapter 4

The Trouble with CONFIDENCE

How would you fill in the blank to the following sentence?

I feel confident when _____.

I posed this question to a special group of women from Wisconsin, and here are some of their responses.

I feel confident when I . . .

- look and feel put-together.
- have practiced.
- know the answer.
- have the ability.
- feel loved and safe.
- have enough sleep.
- feel Jesus' presence.
- don't feel judged.

How did you answer?

What do the responses above say to us?

Often when I ask this question randomly to women, the first response centers around having the right outfit for the right occasion or having a good hair day. We do feel confident when we look good. The question is who are we listening to as we define the "right look"?

The comment about having enough sleep is very practical. The world looks altogether different when we have had an uninterrupted night's rest. What a gift rest is! But sometimes, due to little ones, health issues, or wrestling with life issues, we struggle to find that rest.

Some of the responses above are things we have some control over, such as practicing a presentation, or studying to know the answer, or developing skills needed to accomplish tasks.

Other responses indicate that others influence our ability to feel confident. We may feel judged by what others say or how they respond to us in any given moment. We may feel unloved or unsafe because of a hurtful relationship. Those are often circumstances where we cannot control the situation, though we can control how we respond to those people or conversations.

As I probed deeper to find out why the responses above are important to make us feel confident, I heard concerns such as:

- I don't want to look like a fool or appear to be a failure, so I must work hard to overcompensate for my weaknesses.

- I'm up against some of the best in the business. I have to be at my best to compete with _____! (Much of this is based on comparisons and expectations.)

- I'm a stay-at-home mom. People make comments that I don't work, or I'm wasting my talent, or . . . you've heard the comments.

- I want to be sure that I am doing the right thing—the thing that the Lord would want me to do.

I noticed a series of questions that came up related to confidence:

- Why do we crave it?
- When do we have it?
- Why don't we have it?
- How did we lose it?
- Did we ever have it?

Why is it important that you feel confident?

Before you answer that, how would you define *confident*? There are many misconceptions about what *confidence* actually is (and is not). Let's take a closer look at how it is defined.

Definition of CONFIDENT: con·fi·dent / ˈkänfədənt/

The *Oxford Dictionary* defines the noun as:

- *The feeling or belief that one can have faith in or rely on someone or something.*

    Synonyms: **trust**, belief, faith, conviction

OR

- *The state of feeling certain about the truth of something*

    Synonyms: **sureness**, positiveness, conviction, reliability, assuredness, etc.

- *A feeling of self-assurance arising from an appreciation of one's own abilities or qualities.*

    Synonyms: **self-assurance**, self-confidence, self-reliance, belief in oneself, faith in oneself, positiveness, assertiveness, self-possession, nerve, poise, etc.

- *The telling of private matters or secrets with mutual trust. Or a secret or private matter told to someone under a condition of trust.*

    Synonyms: **secret**, private affair, confidential matter, confidentiality, intimacy

Then I checked the Urban Dictionary. (Sometimes understanding how the word is used in today's culture gives new meaning, though I don't always recommend it.) Here's what they said:

> *A confident woman is <u>SEXXY</u>, but not an <u>egocentric</u> woman. Something initially many younger women struggle with, until she gets older or experiences a jerk.*

Hmm. . . What definition would you use?

Why do we STRUGGLE?

If confidence is based on a self-reliance or self-assuredness, I don't know about you, but I am pretty fickle when it comes to being self-confident. What percentage of your day do you *feel* confident? Most days, if being confident relies on how I *feel*, then the game's over.

Some days I feel confident, even SEXXY confident!

Some days I can pretend to be confident. You know the old expressions *"Fake it until you make it"* and *"Act as if you have it"*?

Both of these imply that by imitating confidence or a positive mindset, we can realize those qualities in our life. Which is true to a point. Our ability to imagine—or play make believe—can often spark in us the exact actions needed to become confident.

Actions seem to follow feelings, but really, both actions and feelings are necessary. If we try to "fake it" without action for very long, we soon begin to develop an imposter syndrome where we doubt our accomplishments and have a persistent growing fear of being exposed as a "fraud."

That is where the first definition of confidence I mentioned earlier comes into play. *The feeling or belief that one can have faith in or rely on someone or something.* If we cannot trust ourselves, or believe in ourselves, we quickly see ourselves as the imposter.

But when we align our actions and our feelings to our personal values and beliefs, we are able to both act and feel confident.

I loved one woman's definition: She said she feels confident when the smile on her face reflects the smile she is feeling inside.

Ah! There it is! **When the external lines up with the internal.** Yes, that feels true. That feels like confidence.

Would you agree?

But for some reason, we tend to not let it be that simple. Instead, we give priority to external things and accept the message that our value depends on . . .

> what we have,

> or what we can do,

> or what people think of what we have or can do.

Think about that. Is that true for you?

Then I also consider if I believe that God made me special. And I believe he is the God of the Universe, my Creator, Master Designer, Life Giver, Blessed Controller, and much more. If he made me, and I am a follower of him, **why do I struggle to believe I can be confident? Why do you?**

I've come to the conclusion, as many have before me, that a large part of the reason we struggle with confidence is that **we are not sure of who we are.** When Jenn asked me about my value, I believed God created me, and I knew a lot about myself, but I didn't really own WHO I WAS.

I knew the roles I played.
I knew the tasks I performed.

But I struggled to accept WHO I was, mostly because I thought I needed to be more like *so-and-so,* who seemed to have it all together. I couldn't be content being me or settle for my way of doing things.

More than not owning our own design, we often struggle with what we know about God. **Do we really KNOW God?**

I knew a lot of things about God. I was a worshiper and a worship leader at my church. I took my relationship with God very seriously. But I had neatly packaged all I knew about God in a nice box and tied it up with a bow, though it wasn't until I looked back over my story that I saw this.

But if confidence is aligning what you truly believe about yourself and God with WHO God really created you to be and WHAT he created you to do, then it's pretty important that I know myself *and* God.

On my 40th birthday, a friend said to me, "*Kathy, if you were a color, you would be bright yellow like the sun.*" I remembered back to my childhood as a second grader feeling that kind of bright and cheery confidence. My husband teased that I was indeed "*always pumping sunshine.*" I wasn't sure that was a compliment, but I loved it.

But what happens when yellow, sunshine-pumping girl comes face-to-face with confidence-destroying events?

I mentioned in Chapter 1 how several events in life caused me to STOP. They all happened during four very difficult years of my life. I experienced loss of confidence when I . . .

- felt like our home and family environment was no longer a safe place.

- developed an autoimmune disease that threatened to affect other organs in my body as well.

- needed to quit the only job I had ever wanted or trained for because of my health and my family situation.

- let go of a lifelong dream of being a pastor's wife, which added a sense of loss of identity and security for both my husband and me.

Why did these events cause me to lose confidence?
Lose heart? *Yes.* Lose courage? *Yes.* But how did this affect my confidence?

Well, for one thing, it meant that in every area of my life, I was forced to take a good, long look at myself and see what was *really* going on. That isn't always easy and most often humbling.

But it also meant that the "comfort zone" I had created for myself was gone. I couldn't find healing in any of these areas if I insisted on keeping things comfortable, which meant I had to find new ways of doing LIFE.

And anytime you have to rethink how to do an old thing or discover completely new ways of living, it has a dramatic effect on your confidence.

But I was hopeful that we were going to be ok! At each stage, I felt like I could see God *working all things for good*. I knew he would not waste this. I still had hope. I still pumped sunshine. This was going to be ok!

By August 2006, our family was beginning to feel life, almost a resurrection of sorts. My husband, Rennie, was smiling again, I was humming again, and our family was turning toward one another instead of away from each other. Ren and I were starting to dream again of what we could do next. It was a special time and year for us.

On one exceptionally beautiful afternoon, our youngest daughter, Leisha, went for walk out on our country road. I met her about a mile from our home. I rolled down the window on my van, then she crossed her arms and tucked her chin on her wrist as she leaned in the door. Her face was flushed from the exercise of her walk. Her eyes sparkled with thoughts and ideas that were skimming around in that beautiful head of hers.

She was dreaming of the day that she would have her driver's permit, which was just weeks away. I teased her, *"You just want power."* I could see the wheels in her mind begin spinning and quite rapidly she replied,

"I don't need power. I want to influence. I want to say, 'I'm going. Come with me!'"

I remember thinking *"Who says that when they are just fifteen?"* I stroked her nose like I had many times since the day of her birth. *"Honey, you were made to influence. I have no doubt about that."*

I offered to take her to the coffee shop to meet her friend, but Abby was already on the way to pick her up on the road. I drove home.

I walked in the door and dropped the mail on the counter, and then the phone rang. It was my neighbor. *"Kathy, Leisha's been hit by a car. Can you come?"*

O God!

Leisha had arrived at the next intersection about the same time Abby did from opposite directions. But Leisha didn't recognize Abby's vehicle, so Abby honked. Leisha looked up, squealed with delight, and ran across the intersection—into the path of a car.

In the dark days that followed, I was unable to be the bright yellow girl that pumped sunshine. No yellow! No sun! I lost confidence in myself and my ability to care for myself or protect my girls or my husband from such awfulness. But what was worse, I lost confidence in God. How could he let this happen?

My mentor, Linda Dillow, wrote, *"Kathy, I don't know how you will do it, but keep talking to your Heavenly Father. Tell him the truth about what you are feeling."*

Oh, I had some things to say to God, alright!

Chapter 5
Taking Lessons from a Psalm

MY THOUGHTS WENT to Psalm 77. I had studied that psalm in detail—in fact, I think it was Linda that had first taught on the passage. But now I read it with different eyes and a broken heart.

I opened my *New Living Translation Bible* with all my notes in the margins. At the beginning of Chapter 77, I had written *HONESTY*.

The Psalmist Asaph wrote very honestly. **He NOTICED what was REAL—what was really going on in his life.**

> I cry out to God; yes, I shout.
> Oh, that God would listen to me!
> **2** When I was in deep trouble,
> I searched for the Lord.
> All night long I prayed, with hands lifted toward heaven,
> but my soul was not comforted.
> **3** I think of God, and I moan,
> overwhelmed with longing for his help.
> **4** You don't let me sleep.
> I am too distressed even to pray!
> **5** I think of the good old days,
> long since ended,
> **6** when my nights were filled with joyful songs.
> I search my soul and ponder the difference now.

I had already spent a great deal of time getting real about my life, health, family, jobs, and dreams. But even those things looked different again from this side of Leisha's death. These words from the Psalmist felt like they were coming from somewhere deep within me, each phrase spilling out of me with bitter sobs.

But the Psalmist didn't stop there. **He also EXPRESSED HONESTLY how he FEELS about God.**

> **7** Has the Lord rejected me forever?
>
> Will he never again be kind to me?
>
> **8** Is his unfailing love gone forever?
>
> Have his promises permanently failed?
>
> **9** Has God forgotten to be gracious?
>
> Has he slammed the door on his compassion?

My version reads something like . . .

> *I worshipped you, I served you, I was humble, I was loving,*
>
> *I tried to have the right attitude.*
>
> *How could you lead me to this place?*
>
> *How can you allow such pain?*
>
> *I tried to serve you the best I knew how.*
>
> *Why would you allow me to hurt like this?*
>
> *Where were you?*

And then I see the Psalmist—with a flair for the dramatic—put the back of his hand to his forehead and say, "*This is my fate; the Most High has turned his hand against me.*"

Overdramatic? Maybe! But that's what feels real at the moment.

If you got honest with God . . .

- What would you have to say about how things REALLY ARE now?

- How does it sound when you have serious conversation with God?
- And what does all this have to do with confidence?

Sometimes when life hits us with both barrels, we wonder where God is in that moment. We might struggle to have confidence in him after a traumatic event. But to tell God how we really feel may cause us to feel ashamed, guilty, or even disrespectful.

Or we might turn both barrels on him in a blast of anger, and then not speak to him again, screaming, *"I'm not ever letting you do that to me again."*

I did all of that. But I was amazed that in the middle of the mess, I sensed God was ok with my honesty. In fact, God invites us to be honest.

> But you desire **honesty** from the womb,
>
> teaching me wisdom even there. **Psalm 51:6**

More than once I found myself sitting on God's lap and not mincing any words. In fact, one particularly bad day, I imagined myself stomping on his feet and beating on his chest until I couldn't beat any more.

The transforming power of that moment was that at the end of the wrestling, where was I? I was in his arms, sobbing with every breath left in me. It was a moment of deepest intimacy that I will never forget.

Had my circumstances changed? NO!

But I had been HONEST with God. I had told him the truth about how I felt, and in doing that, I got the pain out of me. Now we could deal with the mess together.

What do you say to yourself? To God?
What do you need to say?

Too often we stop at being honest. It allows us to get it all off our chest. We feel better and we think we are ready to move on.

But how many times do we get STUCK just telling the same story over and over again.

We find ourselves in a rut that we dig deeper and deeper each time we rehearse the facts as we know them, based on our perspective at the time. (Much like I have done for all these years with my second-grade story.)

We tell the story over and over, but we never really listen to what we are saying. We don't learn from it. We just hear it again and again, until we only remember the STUFF

but not the VALUE of the moment.

Yes, honesty is very important. But if that is where we continue to focus our attention, **what is the probable outcome?**

Come on . . . you know! You've found yourself wallowing in the STUFF that consumes your thoughts and your emotions just like I have. You've become fixed on what can't be fixed. Your thoughts get locked onto all the ways you've been hurt, or abused, or broken. Your emotions get all tangled in the pain, leaving little room for anything else. That leads to discouragement, depression, and anxiety.

Does that sound familiar?

Honesty does play a role in our journey, but we can't stop there.

No, the Psalmist shows us that in these moments, we have an opportunity to **PIVOT:**

> **(NIV) 11** But then I **RECALL** all you have done, O Lord;
>
> I **REMEMBER** your wonderful deeds of long ago.
>
> **12** They are constantly in my thoughts.
>
> I **MEDITATE** on your mighty works.

The Psalmist Asaph chooses to change perspective. His choice allows him to turn from his circumstances and **turn to REMEMBER God!**

And you know what happens next? The Psalmist says **O GOD!**

> **13 O God,** your ways are holy.
>
> Is there any god as mighty as you?

14 *You are the God of great wonders!*

You demonstrate your awesome power among the nations.

15 By your strong arm, you redeemed your people,

the descendants of Jacob and Joseph.

Honesty + Remembering = Intimacy: O GOD, I see you!

When I worked through this process, I looked back at the night Leisha died. I remembered that all I could say that night was O! I didn't even have the capacity to pray *O GOD*. I just prayed O!

I didn't notice that right away. But after
being honest with God about what was REAL and about how I FEEL,
after choosing to PIVOT to remember God,
I saw God at the scene of her accident!

O God!

That's when the Psalmist tells the age-old story. The story that the children of Israel told again and again of that moment when their circumstances put them between a rock and a hard place. And they SAW God!

In fact, the Psalmist tells us that even the Red Sea saw God.

16 When the **Red Sea saw you,** O God,

its waters looked and trembled!

The sea quaked to its very depths.

17 The clouds poured down rain;

the thunder rumbled in the sky.

Your arrows of lightning flashed.

18 Your thunder roared from the whirlwind;

the lightning lit up the world!

The earth trembled and shook.

When the Red Sea saw you, O GOD…

19 Your road led through the sea,

your pathway through the mighty waters—

a pathway no one knew was there!

When Leisha died, **I couldn't imagine** how I was going to get through the pain of that loss. I couldn't see how our family could survive this tragedy. I had no confidence in myself to make it happen.

But I took a risk and kept *"talking to my Heavenly Father."*

- I got honest about what was real and how I felt.
- I chose to pivot from the circumstances to remember, to recall, to meditate on God.
- I saw God, O God, seeing into me. *Into Me See = Intimacy*

My confidence began to grow. I began to trust that he would open a way *through* the grief. I began to see a pathway I could never have imagined!

Our future, our ability to envision our future, our faith, is built on confidence.

What or who are you putting your confidence in?

Blessed are those who trust in the Lord

and have made the Lord their hope and confidence.

Jer. 17:7 NLT

TAKEAWAYS:

Use the next few moments to write down your primary aha moments from PART ONE. Choose one or two insights that seem to stand out from the things you have noticed in these chapters. Jot them down now, so you won't forget. You will be referring back to some of this information as you go through the book.

BUDDY CHECK-IN:

Now is a good time to schedule some time with your buddy to discuss the chapters in this section.

Part Two

How Honest Are You

About YOU?

WE ARE GOING to follow the Psalmist's formula in the following sections of this book.

HONESTY + REMEMBERING = INTIMACY,
which leads to confidence

Part Two starts with being HONEST about
> what's really going on,
> who you are,
> what you were made (in fact, *chosen*) to be and do.

Honesty is not always easy, but neither is pretending life is what it is not. And at the end of pretense, not only are we exhausted, but we've ended up with false conclusions as well.

I invite you to get in a safe space, take a deep breath, and ask the Lord to show you what is REAL. I believe you will be surprised by more beauty and added goodness than you ever imagined.

Ready? Let's get HONEST!

Chapter 6

What's Really Going On?

Being confident is being able to see things as they really are.

THE THING ABOUT *confidence* is that we have times in our story when confidence was evident, and we overcame tremendous odds or achieved great things. We can remember what that felt like and would like to live in that moment again.

While that "old confidence" continues to speak into who we are now,

"What we were, isn't what we are."

I find myself retelling the stories of issues I overcame in those very difficult years. It is true that those moments will always be a part of me, and lessons I learned there continue to affect behaviors and decisions I make today.

But they are not my *now*. They are where I was, who I was.

I must take a good look and get honest about what is really going on—in this day, in these circumstances.

The invitation to stop that we talked about in Chapter 2 gives us a unique opportunity to look around at our current circumstances and to pay attention to what's really true in our life.

What is real? What do you see?

We often struggle to admit our reality because, honestly, we're trying really hard to look good, or at least *good enough*. We may feel inadequate somehow, that we are not doing work that matters now. We overcompensate by making it look like we are more than we truly are.

We want to look the part of the butterfly even when we're still a caterpillar. We put on a masquerade and pretend to be *who and what we are not* to look the part. (Refer back to our discussion of imposter syndrome in Chapter 3.)

Now don't get me wrong. There are days when I don't feel great, or I'm struggling with an attitude or an issue in a relationship. I'm not going to tell everyone what I'm dealing with. I'll put on that outfit that makes me feel beautiful, or at least comfortable, and I'll partner that with my best smile and go out to meet my world. Most of that world doesn't need or even want to know what is going on inside of me.

But if I keep that mask on when I look in the mirror, I can get caught in the pretense of having to live up to something that isn't authentic.

What if we, like the little caterpillar when it is hatched, own the little leaf we have been born on that may feel small and insignificant to

us. For the caterpillar, it is that season in life where she can't go anywhere else. She doesn't have the ability to fly. She just has little, tiny, stocky legs to start with. If she crossed her arms and whined, *"I don't like where I am, so I quit,"* then she would never get any bigger, she would never grow, and she would never develop into a butterfly. She doesn't have a lot of options, but that doesn't stop her.

The beauty of this stage in the caterpillar's life is that this is where the caterpillar does most of her growth in length and weight. She accepts where she lives and her current place in life. Therefore, she does what she needs to do to grow exponentially right there.

As a child, our arms and legs are tiny, our brains are taking in more information than we know what to do with. From the time we are born until we are six or seven years old, we have already begun to create the TRUTH by which we will live—which may or may not be completely true. We make correlations between relationships that are meaningful, how to give and receive love, and what behaviors are acceptable, to name a few.

Often we are taught this TRUTH by our parents or other significant grown-ups who may or may not be living their authentic selves. Unless we choose to pay attention to our own lives, we may be passing on UNTRUTH to yet another generation.

As women living in our current reality, WHAT IF we embraced this place that may seem small and insignificant, where we may feel underappreciated and overworked. WHAT IF instead of fighting against it, instead of trying to bust out of this rut we find ourselves in, we embrace what's real and find the real TRUTH—the whole truth.

Now, my beloved woman, I hear you muttering under your breath, *"That's easy for Kathy to say, but she doesn't know the STUFF I have had to live through."*

You are right! I don't know your specific story. I don't know your stuff unless you tell me.

It often feels like some people have an easy, perfect life. In fact, I would guess that a woman in your world came to mind as soon as you read that last sentence. You see a woman who has it all, while others, like yourself, seem to struggle through every day and every minute. You compare yourself to this "perfect" woman, and her life and family, and wish you could have what she has.

I get it. I have occasionally thought the same thing.

Why does her life get to be easy and mine is hard?

But I have a challenge for you. Name the woman you think has it all figured out, the one who looks like she has put together the perfect life. Now, call her up, invite her out for coffee, and ask her to share her secret with you. My guess is she will choke on her sip of coffee and let out a laugh. She knows her life is far from perfect.

I dare you to intentionally become acquainted with that woman. You may quickly learn that she has her own issues and circumstances to overcome. The old adage that says *"you can't understand someone until you've walked a mile in their shoes"* is true.

That is life. Unless you are the amazing exception and have never had a problem. Of course, those women aren't reading this book.

Before we move on, **what is your REAL—your current reality?**

Let's take a moment to ask ourselves some questions. Grab your workbook and a pen, and consider your answers to the questions I have for you there. Sit back, take a deep breath, and look around at your life.

What do you see?

- What is the condition of your **living environment?**
- What do you notice about **yourself**: your appearance, your shape, your health, things you like and don't like about yourself?
- How do you spend your **time**?
- What **roles** do you play?

It is fine to just make mental notes at this time, but it might be helpful for you to begin writing down what you are noticing to save time later. Part of our transformation comes when we take what is in our brain, send it down our arm through the pen to the page, and then see what we have written and send it back to our brain.

We write things down in order to **SEE what we are noticing** and, therefore, do something about them.

And because I know how this often goes, I invite you to **make two lists:**
- one for the things you see as positive
- and another for the negative.

Both lists are true, but the focus of each list is different.

Spend some time pondering these questions. Come back to the book when you have created your lists.

What do you see?

Which list—positive or negative—are you focusing on the most?

Years ago, I did this exercise as a result of reading a book authored by my mentor Linda Dillow called *Calm My Anxious Heart*[2]. One story Linda shares has stuck with me. Linda tells of a young bride writing a letter full of complaints to her mother about how . . .

> . . .*life was not what she had hoped or expected. When she married her beloved, who was in the Marines, she thought it would be romantic and exciting to live in foreign countries and travel the globe. But two years later, she was lonely and deeply discontented. . . .She had no friends, she couldn't speak the language and figured it wasn't worth the effort to learn since they could be moved from one country to another at a moment's notice. Worst of all, the groom was never home. She ended with "I can't take this any longer. I'm coming home."*
>
> Her astute mother faxed a reply consisting of just two lines.
>
> *"Two women looked through prison bars.*
>
> *One saw mud, the other saw stars."*

Whoa! I remember my breath catching as I looked at my lists after reading this wise momma's reply to her daughter. We all have circumstances or situations that we don't like. They may even appear to be prison bars.

But we each have a choice about how we look at our current reality. We can focus on the mud and get sucked deeper into the negatives. Or we can choose to look up to see the stars and as we do, begin to see the possibilities. (We will talk more about that later.)

For now,

Mud list? Stars list?

Which list are you focusing on most?

BUDDY CHECK-IN:

Take some time to discuss your lists with your buddy.

You might join in to see what others are saying about these lists in the Facebook Community too.

Chapter 7

Are You Accepting WHO You Are?

Being confident is being able to see yourself for who you truly are.

IN CHAPTER 6, I invited you to spend some time in your workbook and pay attention to what is REAL about **yourself**: your appearance, your shape, your health, things you like and don't like about yourself.

Since we are being honest, what is the first thing you think about when discussing your physical shape? *(Did I just see you roll your eyes?)*

Would your first thoughts fit in the mud or the stars list that we spoke of earlier?

I invite you to take a moment in front of a mirror, perhaps in the morning before you get dressed for the day. Take a good, honest look at the physical body that you see.

What are your features that you struggle with most? Let's start there because most often that is the first thing we see. Mud list stuff.

Now, what are the features that you love, the ones that make you feel beautiful? Celebrate those aspects of your beauty.

Next consider that you were CHOSEN by God to be who you are! To look like you do, to act like you do, to be who you are. Flaws and all, asymmetrical body shape and all, weirdnesses and all.

You were CHOSEN TO BE YOU!

I know you know that! But how often do you get STUCK in translating that truth into your thoughts, behaviors, decisions, and attitudes?

My heart keeps coming back to the woman who says,
"I'm chosen to be me? Is THIS a blessing? Or a curse?"

Really, God? You gave others looks, or skills, or this gift or that (fill in the blank). Is this really all the better you could do for me? This doesn't feel like a gift.

As a life coach, I'm in the business of *positive psychology*. In coaching, we focus on the strengths of a person because the work we do there will always make them stronger, better, and more effective. We like to talk about our positives: our traits, strengths, and uniquenesses that make us feel and look confident.

Which is easier for you? To acknowledge what is positive about you or to pick on the negatives? Most of the time, the answer is the negatives—back to the mud list. We get stuck focusing on our weaknesses, faults, or oddities that leave us feeling insecure, embarrassed, or perhaps ashamed.

Why is that? Here are a few of the answers I have gotten from women I coach.

- It takes less work to think of the negatives. I see them first.
- Culture gives us a skewed view of what's expected.
- I know I can do better, be better, look better, _____.
- I don't want to be prideful.
- I feel like I've been lazy, so I start there.
- Easier to bring up the negatives about us before someone else does.
- Because I know a woman who _____. (comparisons)
- Because Satan is a king of lies and plants doubts.

What would your answer be?

We need to remember, when this is our mindset, we focus on the negatives. Our response is to doubt ourselves, calling every part of who we are into question. But even if we spend 100% of our time and energy focusing on improving our weaknesses, those characteristics only become mediocre at best.

When we see the positives of someone else's life and want what they have instead of our own, we need to remember we are comparing our insides (all that we know about ourselves) with their outsides (all that we can see about them, which is what they have chosen to show us).

Again, I encourage you to get to know that "scary" woman. I don't mean they are dark or ominous, or that they make you afraid. Well, ok, maybe they have made you a little afraid. But it is not because they frighten you.

Rather they are, or at least they appear to be, *strong, confident women who are world changers.* They are women we/I admire a great deal. They come from many walks of life. They serve the world in many different ways. But there is something about them that intimidates us. That makes them "scary"!

Yet most often, those amazing women have their own stuff they struggle with. They may be ahead of us in some ways. They may have found victory in areas we still struggle with. But they also know what it is like to feel unsure or insecure. They have scary women in their world, too, remember.

What if we acknowledge each other as the remarkable beings that we are? What if we quit comparing ourselves to one another and start embracing our own remarkable selves?

What would be the benefit to you and to your world if you LOVED yourself unconditionally and ACCEPTED yourself just the way you are?

Let's take a look at what the Bible says about this. You may be familiar with this passage if I read it from *New International translation.*

Scripture: Romans 12:1-3 (NIV)

> Therefore, I urge you, brothers and sisters, in view of God's mercy, to offer your bodies as a living sacrifice, holy and pleasing to God—this is your true and proper worship. **2** Do

not conform to the pattern of this world, but be transformed by the renewing of your mind. Then you will be able to test and approve what God's will is—his good, pleasing and perfect will.

3 For by the grace given me I say to every one of you: Do not think of yourself more highly than you ought, but rather think of yourself with sober judgment, in accordance with the faith God has distributed to each of you.

What does *"think of yourself with sober judgment"* mean to you? Often, I think in terms of a "sackcloth and ashes" kind of humility. This phrase comes to mind every time I hear someone being acknowledged or praised for a job well done and their response is, *"Oh it's not me! It's God!"* I think I know what they mean, but I wonder if they really do. I want to say to that person, *"But God made you to be you! It IS you! Just say thank you for the affirmation!"*

These words *"think of yourself with sober judgment"* follow verse 2 that says, *"be transformed by the renewing of your mind."* Our *"sober judgment"* is to be born out of a renewed mind, from sound thinking.

Now let's read that passage again including more of the context—this time from *The Passion Translation* (TPT). Highlight the WORDS OR PHRASES that stand out to you.

12:1 Beloved friends, what should be our proper response to God's marvelous mercies? I encourage you to surrender yourselves to God to be his sacred, living sacrifices. And live in holiness, experiencing all that delights his heart. For this becomes your genuine expression of worship.

2 Stop imitating the ideals and opinions of the culture around you, but be inwardly transformed by the Holy Spirit through a total reformation of how you think. This will empower you to discern God's will as you live a beautiful life, satisfying and perfect in his eyes.

3 God has given me grace to speak a warning about pride. I would ask each of you to be emptied of self-promotion and not create a false image of your importance. Instead, honestly assess your worth by using your God-given faith as the standard of measurement, and then you will see your true value with an appropriate self-esteem.

4 In the human body there are many parts and organs, each with a unique function. **5** And so it is in the body of Christ. For though we are many, we've all been mingled into one body in Christ. This means that we are all vitally joined to one another, with each contributing to the others.

6 God's marvelous grace imparts to each one of us varying gifts and ministries that are uniquely ours. So if God has given you the grace-gift of prophecy, you must activate your gift by using the proportion of faith you have to prophesy. **7** If your grace-gift is serving, then thrive in serving others well. If you have the grace-gift of teaching, then be actively teaching and training others. **8** If you have the grace-gift of encouragement, then use it often to encourage others. If you have the grace-gift of giving to meet the needs of others, then may you prosper in your generosity without any fanfare. If you have the gift of leadership, be passionate about your leadership. And if you have the gift of showing compassion, then flourish in your cheerful display of compassion.

What jumped off the page for you? Again, I'm wishing we could share thoughts over my dining room table, but this is a great conversation to have with your buddy.

One woman shared, *"If we don't 'think right' about ourselves and love and accept who we really are, then of course we will always be needing to change ourselves or imagine we need to be like someone else."*

Another noticed the phrase *"be inwardly transformed"* and spoke to the awareness that we can make outward changes, but it's the work that we do inside that changes how we think. *That internal change "empowers you to discern God's will as you live a beautiful life, satisfying and perfect in his eyes."*

When I first came across this passage years ago, I latched onto *"Do not think of yourself more highly than you ought"* from the NIV version. I thought that meant I needed to be sacrificially humble, hence the "sackcloth and ashes" comment I made earlier.

What I heard initially was "don't be prideful, don't tell people how good you are," or in my music world, "don't take all the solos."

After my conversation with Jenn Wenzke about whether I knew my value, I was struck by the phrase as it was translated in *The Passion Translation*: *"Honestly assess your worth by using your God-given faith as the standard of measurement, and then you will see your **true value.**"*

As I pondered the true message in the context of this chapter, I saw that right after the author, Paul, makes this statement, he goes on to talk about how we are part of a body of Christ, much like my finger is part of my physical body. We couldn't function with only fingers, or elbows, or eyes. Neither can we can all look alike for the body of Christ to work.

Michele Cushatt, author, speaker, and woman I admire wrote:

> *For too many years, I tried to be someone else. I saw all the ways I was different, and those differences felt an awful lot like flaws. In my mind, I was a problem that needed fixing. And until I could be as put-together as everyone else appeared, I needed to keep a low profile and hide.*

> *What a thrill—and relief—to discover the ocean of God's grace and affection. Buffered by his sufficiency, I learned my differences weren't flaws to fix but offerings to share. And even my most embarrassing weaknesses were a means of revealing God's beautiful mercy. #leveragesj18 [3]*

YOU are WHO you are for a reason! We are different from each other for a reason. Our flaws and weaknesses are as much a part of what we share with our world as our beauty and our virtues. We both are part of something bigger than us when the remarkable truth of who we are is partnered with the amazing designs of others.

Together we complete rather than compete or compare.

How are you doing at assessing yourself? How does accepting WHO YOU ARE honestly and accurately benefit you—and your world?

BUDDY CHECK-IN:

Check in with your buddy and share the strengths you see in one another. Celebrate your differences and how you complete—not compete with—each other.

Chapter 8

What S.H.A.P.E. Are You In?

Being confident is recognizing you have been CHOSEN by God

to be who you are in the body of Christ.

D AN MILLER WRITES, in his book *Wisdom Meets Passion*[4]:

> *When you get to heaven, God is not going to ask you why you weren't more like Mother Teresa, Billy Graham, or Bono. He's likely to ask you why you weren't more like you.... Remember the 1994 movie Forrest Gump? At one part, Jenny asks, "What are you gonna be when you grow up?" Forrest replies, "Why can't I be me?"*

That's the challenge! To discover and accept who we really are. To let our unique talents and personality be authentic and let God use us as he created us to serve our world.

Accepting WHO WE ARE means we need to be HONEST about our S.H.A.P.E. And no, I'm not talking about our physical shapes. Let's elaborate on S.H.A.P.E. by using it as an acrostic to help us identify more fully the design God gave us.

S - Spiritual Gifts (or Grace Gifts as used in Rom 12:6-7)

H - Heart (or Passion)

A - Abilities

P - Personality

E - Experiences

This is not original with me. Rick Warren first used this in his book *Purpose Driven Life*[5]. But over the years, I have found this exercise to be very helpful personally and with my clients as they take a refresher course on WHO AM I 101.

As we go through these aspects of S.H.A.P.E., ask yourself:

- Where am I thinking right?
- Where does my thinking need to be transformed?
- Where am I seeing STARS? Where am I looking at MUD?

Use the workbook to record your thoughts and look for additional resources that may help you with each aspect.

Spiritual / Grace Gifts

It is not my purpose to explore our spiritual gifts, or any of the S.H.A.P.E. aspects, in great detail—though it makes for a great study. If you want to know more about the gifts, you can start by studying 1 Corinthians 12, but here are some things you should remember.

- Spiritual gifts are abilities given to us by God to allow us to make our unique contribution to the world. God chooses the gifts he gives to us. 1 Cor 12:28-31 and in 1 Cor 14:12-13

- We often are given spiritual gifts at the time of our salvation, or spiritual birth. But there are verses that indicate we can receive them later as well.

- Every believer has at least one Spiritual Gift. There is no right or wrong Gift.

  To look deeper into the kinds of Spiritual Gifts that God gives, look at: 1 Corinthians 12:8-10, 28, Romans 12: 6-8 Ephesians 4:11, 1 Peter 4:9-10.

But it is important to keep Romans 12:6-8 in mind. Here is Kathy's version:

  God's marvelous grace imparts to each one of us varying gifts and ministries that are **uniquely ours. If God has given you a grace-gift** (spiritual gift) . . .

which he has . . .

USE IT!

If it's prophecy, activate it.

If it's serving, then thrive in serving.

If it's teaching, actively teach and train.

If it's encouragement, then use it often.

If it's giving, then prosper in your generosity.

If it's leadership, be passionate about your leadership.

If it's showing compassion, then flourish in your gracious display of compassion.

What is your spiritual gift? What does it look like to use your gift in your world?

Look for resources to help you in the workbook.

Heart / Passion

This is your "heartbeat," the God-given desires or passions that point you to areas where you want to make a difference.

Warren writes, *"Physically each of us has a unique heartbeat. Just as we have unique thumbprints, eye prints, voice prints, our hearts beat in slightly different patterns... In the same way, God has given each of us a unique emotional "heartbeat" that races when we think about the subjects, activities and circumstances that interest us. We instinctively care about some things and not about others. These are clues to WHERE you should be serving."* (5Purpose Driven Life, pg 238)

As we discussed this, my friend Cheryl S. pointed out that the things that form your heartbeat, or your passion, will—by necessity—be different from what others experience and value. Too often we feel our differences mean we are flawed, when in reality they are, as Michelle Cushatt's quote said in the last chapter, our offerings to share.

Listen to your heart and consider:

- What are the things that make up your heartbeat, the things you feel strongly about?

- What are the topics that you could stay up all night talking about?

- What are the needs you see? Don't assume everyone sees the same things you do and are just not doing anything about it. I always told my girls, *"If **God gives you eyes to see it**, he probably gave you the ability to do something about that too."*

Abilities

We were born with natural talents and abilities that are also God-given, which makes them just as important as your spiritual gifts. But your abilities you have had since birth. These speak to WHAT you were made to do.

When you are considering your abilities, think about:

- Your strengths—these are things that may seem ordinary to you, but you seem to do it well, and others affirm that.

- Things you do no matter what role you are in.

- How you influence people, build relationships with people, and how you get work done or think.

In her book *You're Already Amazing[6]*, Holley Gerth suggests answering these questions to help determine your STRENGTHs:

Service: Does it help me serve God and others?

Time: Has it been present throughout much of my life?

Relationships: Do others see this?

Energy: Do I feel energized when I'm living this way?

Natural: Does this come naturally to me most of the time? Or do I know God has intentionally developed this in me even though it doesn't come naturally?

Glory: Does God ultimately get the glory from it?

Trials: Even in hard times, does it usually come through somehow?

Heart: Does this really feel like a core part of who I am?

Another resource that that I highly recommend is the Strengths Finder 2.0[7]

Personality / Style

If your Heart tells you WHERE you will make your difference, and your Abilities tell you WHAT you will do, your Personality/style tells you **HOW** you will use your spiritual gifts and abilities.

Personalities remind us that God likes variety. He made some of us to be outgoing while others are more reserved. He made some to be thinkers and others feelers. Some are lovers of routine and structure while others prefer variety and changing things up often.

It may seem that you behave spontaneously with random variations to circumstances around you, but actually your conduct is quite orderly and consistent to you.

The DISC Profile[8] and the Myers-Briggs Inventory / Jung Personality Assesment[9] are two that I recommend. Check the workbook for some free resources that may be helpful for you in this area.

Experiences

Now I know we have only done S.H.A. & P. of our S.H.A.P.E. acrostic. But we are going to give the E (our Experiences or story) its own chapter(s). But before we go to our story, I would like you to think about one more aspect of your life.

Roles

(I know this makes our word S.H.A.P.E.(R.), but the "R" is important, and I didn't want to leave it until after we discussed the E.)

If you were honest about the ROLES you play in your life, what would they be and how many do you have? We talked about this a little in Chapter 6. You might want to refer back to your notes from that chapter.

Your roles might be wife, mom, daughter, sister, friend, boss, employee, co-worker, volunteer, chairperson, etc. These might be roles you have chosen, or you may be in roles you neither asked for, nor wanted, nor can escape without long-term, painful repercussions. If that is true, you may really struggle with exercise.

One woman responded harshly, but honestly, *"I'm putting my time and energy into surviving and making sure my family survives. There isn't any space for anything else."*

Please know, if this is your experience, you may need to take a look at Part Five and address more of your STUCK places before you are ready to move forward here. Please hear me: That's ok! We are starting this process with honesty about what our reality is. We need to grieve some of those spaces before we are ready to move forward elsewhere.

We will talk more about roles in the chapters to come, but for now, I invite you to just take an honest look at where you are spending the majority of your time and energy. We are most effective with only six or seven roles at a time. You will find if you have more than that, you are not effective in all of them. Are you investing yourself in the things that matter most to you?

In your workbook, identify the six or seven roles that are most important to you. As you do, name the key relationships that are important to the role you play.

What have you learned so far in our brief look at your S.H.A.P.E.(R.)?

More importantly, are you aware of the places you are thinking right about yourself and, therefore, interpreting yourself correctly?

By the way, remember that scary woman that you admire greatly, that you think has it all together and that intimidates you? The one you compare yourself to in your church or community and then pronounce yourself to be lacking?

STOP THAT! Isn't it exhausting?

Yes, she has strengths in her S.H.A.P.E. There are things that she does amazingly well. But she has her weaknesses too. That is why she needs you to be you in her life. Have you ever thought about that?

Where do you need to transform your thinking?

> **TAKEAWAYS:**
>
> *Use the next few moments to write down your insights from PART TWO. You will continue to build on some of this information as you go through the book. It is invaluable to capture your new awarenesses as you are working through the material. Good time to check in with your buddy and share with each other what you have learned.*

Part Three

How Honest Are You About Your Story?

HONESTY + REMEMBERING = INTIMACY,
which leads to confidence

So how did it feel to get honest in Part Two about
> what's really going on,
> who you are,
> what you were made (in fact, chosen) to be and do?

I know it's not easy to do, but I hope that something you learned there will give you the confidence to take this next step.

Being HONEST about your real story and what it is telling you about
> what's really going on,
> who you are,
> what you were made (in fact, chosen) to be and do.

OK! I can hear you already beginning to pull back.

Does the thought of looking at your REAL STORY—digging into your past and some of the hard times and hard relationships—seem daunting? I mean, it's behind us, right? It's water under the bridge. We are the authors of our future story, so let's move on with life! Isn't that the best way to step toward our dream, our vision for our life?

Well, yes, but only if you are not dragging your past with you like a ball and chain, allowing it to weigh you down at every turn.

You can't rewrite the past, but you can change the hold it has over you. Isn't it worth taking another look at how your past might be tied to your future?

Deep breath! Now let's see what you find.

Chapter 9

What's Your REAL STORY?

Being confident is telling the truth about your story.

Experiences

OUR EXPERIENCES ARE the events and relationships in our lives that have affected us in some pretty tremendous ways, both positively AND negatively. Most often they leave us with messages that we carry with us for the rest of our lives, messages that replay over and over again when certain scenarios or phrases trigger an emotional response. When those emotions flare up, especially over something that seems to be trivial, it's a pretty clear sign that something in our past is tied to those words or actions. We are still being impacted by those messages, and they are influencing decisions for our future.

Our unique, God-given S.H.A.P.E. is developed through experiences in our storyline. The combination of both S.H.A.P.E. and STORY form the basis of our emotional scripts, the lens through which we view life. Believe me! Embracing the transformation of our emotional scripts is an intense study all of its own. I highly recommend a powerful study by Becky Harling called *Rewriting Your Emotional Script: Erase Old Messages, Embrace New Attitudes*[10].

Becky writes:

> *The thought patterns and attitudes that flow out of our scripts often dictate our responses and reactions. However,*

as we grow up, our original, God-given emotional scripts are often warped by the messages that our experiences, our circumstances, and the voices of significant people have written on our hearts. These scripts become the screenplays for our lives, dictating our responses and reactions.

Some of those events (messages) happened to us as a young child, and we were not able to process whether they were right or wrong, good or bad, let alone their effect on our lives. However, we took that message with us.

For instance, earlier I shared a recurring phrase I've been carrying that immediately shuts me down emotionally: the words "You are not good enough!" When I hear that phrase, or anything similar to it, I catch myself believing the message and responding to it as if it were truth.

When I began the journey of identifying how that message has impacted me over the years, I recalled that I have responded to this phrase as a mom, as a young wife, in college, in high school, and especially in junior high. I was surprised to discover the root of that message occurred all the way back in the second grade. (See Chapter 3 to refresh the story.)

So, what happened when I took the time to record those memorable events on a timeline of my life?

- Well, for one thing, I was able to trace the source of my emotion tied to the words "not good enough."

- I recognized that what I had internalized as a second grader's truth is (and was then) a lie,

- which allowed me to reframe not only the impact of the message in my life but the ache that came with it. The grip of those words lessened.

- Since then, I have been able to replace the lie with truth and move forward without bringing the old response along with me.

Each of us has pages or entire chapters of our lives that we would like to rewrite. Maybe we're afraid that we will never be able to get beyond the hard stuff. But when we take the time to look back at the earlier chapters of our stories, we allow God to help us identify those places that have hurt us deeply; those places threaten to keep us enslaved and hold us back from reaching the dream planted in our hearts. As we notice what those messages are, we can learn from them, reframe them, and move forward in confidence.

Another benefit of looking at my timeline and creating a life map was I discovered other stories in my life that also spoke into my confidence journey.

Miss Lipscomb County

At the end of the school year in 1974 when I was almost 16, I was approached by the coordinator of the local Miss Lipscomb County pageant to be part of the county's Fourth of July celebration. I had grown up watching Miss America and Miss USA pageants, and had often dreamed of being the one on whom they placed the crown. But I said, "No, thank you!"

The chairwoman of the pageant committee was of the persistent sort. She finally said to me, a bit exasperated, *"Kathy, why not?"* I said, *"I'm not good enough."*

Actually that's not what I said. I used words like, *"I'm a preacher's kid, and preacher's kids don't do that kind of stuff."* Honestly, I didn't think they did. But as I looked back, I realized I was saying *"I'm not good enough."* I wonder where that came from?

But the pageant chairwoman took the matter to my parents by the time I got home from school. *"What do you think God wants you to do about the pageant?"* Dad asked. I gulped! Dad wasn't often the one to ask those questions. I usually had these discussions with Mom.

"Well," I stammered. *"I understand that as a preacher's kid that I can't do it."* Dad suggested we pray about it. Oh of course, we pray about it. Then we say no!

Two weeks later, Dad questioned me as to what I thought I would do. I sheepishly said I understood I shouldn't do it. Though honestly, I don't think I really prayed about it. I was pretty sure I already knew the answer.

"Well, your mother and I think that you should. We feel God is opening doors for you here! We think you should fill out the papers and get going."

I'm not sure what I looked like at that moment. My chin must have dropped to the floor and my eyes bugged out as my parents smiled at each other. You didn't have to tell me twice. If God said yes, and my parents heard it, it must be important.

I immediately regretted that I had given back the forms that day of my initial conversation with the chairwoman. Just as quickly, my mom handed me everything I needed to get registered.

That was the day my parents *and* that persistent pageant chairwoman became my heroes. They saw beyond the idea of the beauty pageant to the heart of a young girl. A girl that was hiding behind the mask of being a preacher's kid instead of being honest and saying I didn't feel *"good enough"* to take that giant step. Their belief in me was the beginning of learning to believe in myself and in the intimate involvement of the God who created me.

That insight was a life-changing moment for me! God showed up in my story! I felt confident. I thoroughly enjoyed every minute of it.

But the lesson continued. The moment came for the announcement of the top five finalists. I was pretty sure who all would make it. I had them all picked out.

Even in the middle of all my thoughts, I suddenly became aware that they had called the name of the fifth finalist. Slowly it dawned on me that it was my name. *Kathy Thiessen! That was me! They called my name!*

I felt frozen in place. The girl next to me reached over to give me a push forward. I had not even dared to think this might be a possibility. Yet here I stood, waiting for the judge's question that could decide my fate. His question was pretty simple. *"If you could be anyone living in the world today, who would you be?"*

I quickly thought through a long list of people that I could probably say, and after what seemed like minutes instead of seconds, I said the one thing I knew for sure. *"My mom!"* I gave a lot of reasons to appreciate and admire my mom, at the top of which was her patience in putting up with me getting ready for this event.

As I walked back to my place, I shook my head and mumbled to myself, *"Can't imagine that's going to win me any crown!"*

Then the moment came! I didn't care that I would be the first name called as fourth runner-up. I went from feeling like I was not good enough to becoming a finalist. That meant a lot to me.

But they called the name of the fourth runner-up, and it wasn't me. I was a bit dazed. They called the third and second runners-up and again, it wasn't me. Suddenly, it occurred to me that I was standing next to the girl with the hairdo fit for a crown, holding hands, scarcely able to breathe.

"And the first runner-up is . . ." —it wasn't me! I was shocked!

How is it that an ordinary girl, a preacher's daughter to boot, could win an event that by its very nature said "you're special"? Never in my wildest dreams did I imagine that I would feel that way as MISS LIPSCOMB COUNTY 1974.[1]

Why did I tell you this story with such detail? Was it to let you would know that I'm somebody important? No! To the rest of the world, this was no big deal.

But for me, it was a God moment. I can, even after all these years, recite back to you every minute detail of that event—not just the pageant but of details that brought me to that moment.

That's because God broke into my world. He connected with one of the few dreams I had ever spoken outright: to be a Miss Somebody. I know it is not Miss America, but at 16, I felt like it was.

I saw God take all the loose ends of my young life and tie them together in that event. He showed up in a way I would notice.

I NOTICED that God was not only identifying a false message I had believed since I was young, but he was replacing it with the truth that he had made me special. *"Kathy, Honey—you are more than enough. I want you to be noticed so you can point others to me."*

Does that mean all the other girls were not special? Absolutely not! But at that moment in my story, he chose to use this to speak to me.

What is that story in your life that ties some of your loose ends together?

Take a moment to jot down some of your defining moments in your workbook.

Chapter 10

How to Listen to Your Story

Being confident comes from learning to listen to your story.

OST OF MY life I have felt quite ordinary. I have built a world around me that's comfortable, yet I have sensed a BIG LONGING continue to nudge me to take the next step to a new place. Not just any place though—to that dream that God planted in me at my birth. To that "thing" I was made to do.

Ever felt ordinary? I invite you to consider the story of your life— the REAL story. It's a sequence of events meandering through highs and lows, and messages like *not good enough* and *more than enough*.

Throughout these events, we have people that have impacted us by their amazing lives. Many of them left their mark on us for good, some not. Some parts of our story we love to tell, and we can remember every minute detail. Other parts, not so much. Still others we'd like to erase and rewrite all together. But . . . it's the story we've been given. It's part of what makes us who we are.

A tool I have used to help me get some perspective on my storyline is called a life map. This material is, again, not original to me, although I have come to own the process as I walk through understanding my own story or help others to listen to theirs.

Life Story[11] is a curriculum developed at *Dallas Theological Seminary* for its Spiritual Formation program, under the guidance of the *Center for Christian Leadership*. More information regarding that

75

particular source, and others, can be found in the Resource page of the workbook.

As you begin to look at your *Life Story*, consider the impact of 4-H's:

1. **HERITAGE:** those things that are part of your life strictly because of when, where, and to whom you were born.
2. **HIGH POINTS:** transformational, pivotal events that you celebrate.
3. **HARD TIMES:** transformational, pivotal events that you grieve.
4. **HEROES (or un-heroes):** people who have influenced your life for good or bad.

I have included a chronological timeline in the workbook to help you work through this process. I recognize that our lives are much more dynamic than the linear line our life map at first suggests. However, this is a starting point for identifying those events that are much more than random events.

You have started a list of some of the defining moments already in the last chapter.

- They are, indeed, moments where God gathers all the loose ends of our life and knots them together.
- They point us to SEE where God is and has been working in our story.
- They reveal to us who he made us to be and the difference we are made to make.

But another benefit to listening to our stories is that, when we take time in the good days to SEE what God has already done, we are able to draw on that awareness in the crisis points. That helps us trust that God was working in the hard stuff as well. It gives us strength to believe in the darkness what we knew to be true in the light. That in itself is a powerful motivation to work through this life map process.

Michelle N. had this to say after working on her life map:

> *I've especially been focusing on the Heroes and High Points because I think they've often gotten buried in my past. The*

*Hard Times and the Un-heroes created a heavy shadow that hid the many ways that God was working through my past. **It's like opening a gift as I remember his goodness.** :) And it's been encouraging (and humbling) to be reminded that my life was never as bad as I thought it was in those moments (and even after). Yes, there were some hard times, but God brought heroes to shine through the darkness!*

I invite you to take a look at your story using this life map process. But before you start, there are a few things you need to keep in mind.

1. ***This recounting of your story is in first person.*** It's your story, it's your perspective. Sure, your mom and dad, your siblings, or your spouse are part of the story—as is your teacher, your best friend, and many others. But we are not interested in their perspective at this time.

   YOU are telling YOUR story. This is how YOU saw it. It is your perspective of how these people/events affected you.

2. ***In telling your story, it is important that you are honest about what happened.*** As much as you would like to rewrite the story to look like the good guy who never messes up, that is most likely not true.

   My word to you is, if you want to write fiction, write fiction. But if you want to discern what your own story is truly telling you and see where God is really working, speak truth.

3. ***Invite God into this journey!*** He created you! He's been here from the beginning, whether you knew it or not. He knows about all the days ordained for you (Psalm 139).

   I promise that you will be in awe of the beauty of your real story. Even with tragedy woven throughout, as you are honest with God, God will be honest with you. He will help you remember events or people he placed in your life to give hope. He will help you peel back the layers—layer after layer—revealing areas that need to be addressed in order for you to move forward. He wants you to know who you are meant to be, and even who you are *not* meant to be, and more importantly, how intimately involved he is with your life.

Our past is where the most fundamental definitions of life are made known to us, such as knowing who we are and more importantly, who God is! That is why scripture says over and over again, from Genesis to Revelation, *"do not forget"* and *"remember."* The Psalms are full of such declarations of their authors: *"I will remember your mighty acts."* or *"I will not forget."*

Yet, how many of us truly take time to reflect and learn from the past? We become consumed with the present, and it *is* important to be present in the present.

But it is also true that we can become consumed with our past. It is invaluable to CHOOSE to remember; to make the effort to SEE and LEARN what our own story is telling us.

> Life's answers don't always live in the amount of knowledge we can accumulate. The secret is found in our ability to learn from our significant experiences and change as a response to those moments. Jesus will show you how. By making the choice to remember our story, to be honest about what we see, and to invite God into the process, we give ourselves the opportunity to learn from the past and be transformed by our response to it.
>
> —Mike Breen, *Kairos, Continuous Breakthrough* [12]

Before you go on, why not take time right now to invite your Creator to join you!

I am your creator. You were in my care even before you were born.

Isaiah 44:2

> **BUDDY CHECK-IN:**
>
> *Touch base with your accountability buddy. This is not an easy task, though it can be fascinating. You will need each other's support.*

Chapter 11

Listening to What Your Story Is Telling You

Being confident is born out of learning the lessons from our past.

We are made wise, not merely by the recollection of our past,
but by our responsibility for our future.

—George Bernard Shaw

A s I LOOK back over my life, I realize that my story really isn't about me. Oh, I am the lead character, just as you play lead in yours, but our stories are really about where God shows up. He's really the main character of our story, even as we continue to make decisions and choices as the author.

As we step back from this life map exercise, we begin to notice what really is happening, and we reflect on what God has been doing; this is the fifth "H": HIS HAND. When we look at the big picture of our story, we begin to notice his fingerprints on our everyday, ordinary lives, especially the painful areas that may still leave us paralyzed in some way. Many times just "noticing" will allow us to reframe them and their effects on our future!

A note of caution: Just because you are making a conscious effort to remember, it does not necessarily mean you are gaining insight. It could be that you are simply "preserving" memories which can have tremendous value as we pass stories on to our children and grandchildren. That's true.

But . . . recalling an event invites us to not only gain insight but do something with what we've learned.

Kairos

As we look at the storyline of our lives, we most often see significant events, relationships, or messages in some chronological time frame or sequential order. The word chronological comes from the word *chronos.* However, there is another word used for time, and it is *kairos* (pronounced KY-ross).

We see *kairos* in the first chapter of the book of Mark in his telling of the story of Jesus. Mark's opening scene is with John the Baptist, who is preaching and baptizing, and all the while he is saying, *"After me will come one more powerful than I . . ."*

And Jesus does come to John and asks John to baptize him. As Jesus comes up out of the water, a voice comes from heaven, *"You are my Son, whom I love, with you I am well pleased."* (Mark 1:4-13)

Right after that significant event in Jesus' life, Mark tells us that the Spirit sent Jesus into the desert for forty days. It was during this "hard time," this desert time, that Jesus is tempted by Satan. He returns to Galilee after John the Baptist is put in prison. Mark says Jesus is *"proclaiming the Good News of God."*

Now notice this:

- Jesus experienced a high point—his baptism and the voice affirming who he is.
- Jesus experienced a hard time—a desert time because he had no food and water and Satan was tempting him.

When he comes back, Jesus says,

> "The time has come. The kingdom of God is near.
> Repent and believe the good news!" **Mark 1:15**

First, he declares *"the time has come,"* which means the *kairos* is here! A kairos is defined as *"an event, or an opportunity—a moment in time when perhaps everything changes because it is the right time."*

Time is right for . . . what?

In the second declaration, *"For the . . . kingdom of God to be near!"* Jesus is telling the people in his world the conditions are right in this moment for God's kingdom to break into their world.

We have already identified that the life map on which we will be working is using *chronos* time: a chronological, sequential passing of time. Chronos is our calendar or wristwatch time.

But what we are identifying now on our life maps are *kairos* moments. These are moments when *"the time was right"* for something bigger to happen. These are moments when *chronos time* stands still. These were opportunities for growth simply because everything was right for it.

Imagine! The eternal God *is breaking into your circumstances with an event that will gather all the loose ends of your life and knot them together in his hands.* [13]

Jesus broke into recorded human history at a specific time and place. He walked the roads, he had relationships, and he paid his taxes. He really lived!

Throughout the Gospel accounts, he often asks *"What do you see?"* He would take his disciples or someone with him by the elbow and ask, *"What do you notice? What's really happening?"*

Jesus had kairos moments. His experience on the cross impacted all of humanity for all of eternity. Chronological time has never been the same since.

How is Jesus breaking into your world today?

What *kairos* moments are you noticing? What event in your past is of significance to you, good or bad? Perhaps it is something that changed your life, that broke into the sequence of *chronos* time.

What do you remember about that event?

What feelings, positive or negative, do you have about that experience?

We remember the smallest details about our wedding day, the birth of our child, or that moment of recognition for a job well done. The same is true for moments of tragedy and crisis. I have told you the minute details of my second-grade truth, and the Miss Lipscomb County pageant, and the events surrounding my daughter's death. I remember the entire day, what I did, where I was, who was with me, and what they were wearing.

I'm sure you have moments like that too! Why? Because *kairos* moments are events that stand out as significant to our story, and they are rarely neutral. They leave a tremendous mark on us. They stir up emotions that signal tremendous opportunities for growth. Many times, it is the hard places in our story, the negative events producing negative emotions, that offer us some of the greatest potential for growth.

There is much more we could learn about *kairos*. For now, I invite you to be aware of these moments that stand out in your memory as being life changing in some way. They are not that way by coincidence.

God is at work in your story.

Do you remember how the writer, Asaph, closed Psalm 77? It was by recalling a HUGE *kairos* moment that the children of Israel experienced at the Red Sea.

This is a story Moses tells in great detail in the book of Exodus. It is the story that is told over and over throughout the Old Testament. There is much to Moses' story that I would love to share with you, but I want to focus on the moment Asaph describes at the Red Sea.

> *I talk a lot more about Moses in Chapter 15 of* Lovely Traces *of Hope[1], but I encourage you to read the book of Exodus for yourself to get the whole story.*

Moses has just gone to the Egyptian Pharaoh and told him to let the children of Israel leave rather than to remain slaves in Egypt. Instead of listening to Moses, Pharaoh made the Israelites work harder than ever. Then God showed up with ten plagues which...well, you will just have to read about on your own. (Check out Exodus.)

After a long series of requests, the Egyptian Pharaoh finally gave permission for the children of Israel to leave. But shortly after they left, he changed his mind and ordered his army to pursue the Israelites and bring them back—or worse, kill them.

Picture trying to move an entire community of people, only to have the whole army of Egypt with chariots and horses after you! It would be quite easy for them to catch up to men, women, children, all the livestock and animals carrying all the silver and gold that the Egyptians had given them, plus all of their clothes and baggage and flat bread. (Want to know why? Read Exodus!)

At one point, Moses and the children of Israel are trapped. The Red Sea is in front of them, the Pharaoh and his armies are close behind. For the Israelites, it had to feel like all hope was lost. The extreme emotions they must have felt—one moment rejoicing that they are free, the next exhausted in the journey, and then terrified that they will soon be overtaken and destroyed.

They had prayed, yes. But they were people like you and me. They had to wonder at that point if God would show up.

They wanted to throw up their hands and run. But Moses tells them:

> "Don't be afraid. Just stand still and watch the Lord rescue you today. The Egyptians you see today will never be seen again. The Lord himself will fight for you. Just stay calm."
> **Exodus 14:13-14**

Then God shows up!

> He instructed Moses to raise his staff over the waters to divide the sea. Moses stretched out his hand over the sea, and all that night the Lord drove the sea back with a strong east wind and turned it into dry land. The waters were divided, and the Israelites went through the sea on dry ground, with a wall of water on their right and on their left. **Exodus 14:21-22**

Imagine standing on the edge of that water bank!

The waters trembled and quaked and stood to create a path through the sea, a path no one knew was there (Ps 77:19). Even though they were in the middle of a miracle as the waters stood up to make a way for them, what courage it must have taken to walk with their children by their side between the walls of water, wondering if the wind storm might end at any moment. And this was no flat path. The Red Sea was deep and wide at points. Where they actually crossed is a discussion for another time. But the point is this was not an easy trip.

Yes, the Egyptians were pursuing them and to not cross would be certain death, or undoubtedly the bondage they had just been freed from. Yet even with all the uncertainty, going through the sea appeared to be the least frightening choice.

All night long, the entire tribe of Israelites walked, getting all of the people through to the other side and watching as Pharaoh's horses and chariots and horsemen followed them into the path. You wonder what the children of Israel were thinking. (*What would you have been thinking?*)

But just before daybreak, as the last of the Israelites stepped out on the other side, the Lord told Moses to stretch out his staff over the sea again, and the sea went back into place. The Pharaoh's entire army was swept into the sea. Not one of them survived[1].

That's the Red Sea moment. That's a *kairos moment*.

The Red Sea moment isn't significant because they found themselves between a rock and a hard place. It is significant because at an intense hour where heart-racing fear threatened to paralyze them, God showed up! His presence had never been so real to them.

Even though they had some really good reasons to be afraid, they had some even better reasons to be confident. Over and over in this Exodus story, the Israelites see God show up in ways they could never imagine. Prior to the Red Sea moment, they had endured ten plagues through which God protected them. God showed up once with a cloud to protect them, another time it was fire to light their way. Many times they saw God prepare the way for them.

Now, here in this moment, as Moses raises his staff and the waters SEE GOD, as Asaph tells us in Psalm 77, this whole nation of people take that enormous step of faith and travel through a path of trembling waters.

They put their confidence in God, and he proved to be big enough. No wonder this is the story that is remembered over and over again, told from one generation to the next. All through scripture you see references to the Red Sea. God showed up differently than they had ever seen him before and provided something they all needed but no one could fathom. That's a story you tell your kids and they pass on to their children.

Leisha's death was a Red Sea moment for me!

I tell her story again and again. I relive the memories of her birth, her death, and her life. I refer to the day she died as if it marked the beginning of a new calendar; time before Leisha's death, and time after Leisha's death.

This is my God moment I remember over and over. My Red Sea!

I also connect with the Red Sea moment because I didn't know how I was going to get out of the grief tunnel any more than the children of Israel knew how they were going to get out of Egypt, or get through the Red Sea. God had to show up! And he had to show up differently than he ever had before.

And he did! That's the story I tell.

What's your Red Sea moment? What is the story you share with your world?

Out of our story comes this opportunity to tell, not just a story about our accomplishments, or even our suffering.

- It is the telling of how God was, is, and will ever be present in our lives.

- It is the story of how God showed up in the middle of it all to redeem us.

Where did God show up for you?

Chapter 12

What if You Don't SEE God in Your Story?

Being confident comes from learning to notice God in your story.

A BROKEN WOMAN cautiously peered up at me with a look of concern as she asked me this question. My heart broke for her as she relayed a story of fear and abuse that no young child should ever have to know. Where was God when the man she knew as father became the villain in her story? As an adult she was a "believer" in God, but her heart struggled to reckon what she heard about God with how she felt toward him for abandoning her as a small child.

She felt shame, not because of the story she kept hidden from the world but because she couldn't get over her anger at God. Where was he when she needed him?

That is one of the hard questions that we may never get answered.

For a time after Leisha died, I felt that God had abandoned me or my daughter. Where was he when Leisha approached that intersection? Why didn't he cause her to stop and look before she ran out in front of a car? A few seconds could have made all the difference.

I thought God should have spared her.

Or he could have protected her to begin with.

Or . . . I guess what I wanted was not to hurt so badly myself.

God, where were you?

Scripture tells us that just because we don't see him, doesn't mean God's not there.

> Jesus said to his disciples ". . .And be sure of this: I am with you always, even to the end of the age." **Matthew 28:20**

> For God has said, "I will never fail you. I will never abandon you." **Heb 13:5**

One of my favorite passages is Isaiah 43:1:

> But now, **this is what the Lord says—**
> **he who created you,** Jacob,
> **he who formed you,** Israel:
> **"Do not fear, for I have redeemed you;**
> **I have summoned you by name; you are mine.**

> **2** When you pass through the waters,
> **I will be with you;**
> and when you pass through the rivers,
> they will not sweep over you.
> When you walk through the fire,
> you will not be burned;
> the flames will not set you ablaze.

> **3** For **I am the Lord your God,**
> the Holy One of Israel, your Savior. . ."

Not only does the Lord remind you that he created you and formed you in the womb, but he also redeemed you and called you by your name.

Yes, he confirms that you will have hard times that make you feel like you are drowning. There will be times when you feel like you—

and your values, and passions, and dreams—are being burned by people you care about and situations you thought would turn out differently.

But in the middle of those hard, discouraging moments, he says . . .

"I will be with you."

If that is true . . . where was he? Where is he now?

> He takes us by the elbow, urging us to "Look! Listen!"
> What we expect to see may profoundly affect
> what we actually perceive.
> It is important that we intentionally take time to reflect on what it is
> we are actually seeing. We have a God who constantly calls us to pay
> attention, to observe closely.
>
> — Luci Shaw, *God With Us*[14]

I began to look for him in the middle of my hard times. Oh, my friend, I know he is hard to see sometimes. For one thing, God often shows up in ways we don't expect to see him. He doesn't look like we think God would look. We miss any clues it might be him.

Or his presence doesn't change our situation like we want it to or the way we think God would help us. Again, we miss him.

I invited the woman who couldn't see God in her story to go back to that event when she first felt abandoned by God. **What if he was there and she just hadn't seen him?**

She courageously closed her eyes and let her mind take her back to the night that was dark, to the bed that was hers, to the room that was unsafe. She remembered in vivid detail the sights, the sounds, the smells of that moment. She wept as she described how she felt: alone, frightened, unsafe.

As she began to narrate the events of that night, I asked her to look around for Jesus in that room. *"No, I don't see him. He's not here."*

She continued to recount details of her father, his movements, his.... *"Wait!"* she gasps. *"Ah, there he is. He was there. I didn't see him because I was afraid, but Jesus was there. Right beside me on my bed, holding my hand, his other arm wrapped around me."*

She opened her eyes and stared into mine. *"Kathy, he was there all along. I just didn't see him."*

We wept together.

We went on to speak of other hard questions such as *"Why didn't he stop my dad?"* and *"Why didn't he give me a father that loved me?"*

But something had changed in her. *"All this time I have felt alone in that place, and God was there all the time. He was with me in that awful place. His heart had to be broken that my father was hurting me this way. If he was present with me then, I can trust that he is with me now."*

A few weeks later, I received a note from her saying that she had told her story to her mom and her sisters. They were able to courageously look into their own stories to find some healing. They wanted me to know they were seeing God show up in some unfathomable ways in the everyday moments too.

I don't know what your views are of God, or your relationship to him. But, my friend, he cares deeply for you and for the things that matter to you. Sometimes you have to let go of the story you thought would be your life and learn to find joy in the REAL you are living.

Author Carol Kent writes:

> *The world wants you to be self-confident, to believe that you have what it takes to flourish in uncertain times based entirely on your own abilities. Confidence in yourself has huge limitations, but confidence in the Lord gives you something solid to stand on, because you can fully depend on Him. When you have self-confidence, you believe you can do anything you set your mind to. But with God-confidence, the burden for success doesn't rest on you. As you develop confidence in Him, you'll learn how to turn fear into faith and how to exchange shyness for boldness. #HeHoldsMyHand[15]*

Where is God showing up in your story?

BUDDY CHECK-IN:

I know this part of your story may be very personal to share with your buddy, but I encourage you to do so. Together you can encourage each other to see God in new places and different ways than you have ever seen him before.

I would love to hear from you too. Please come to the Facebook group and leave me a message. How is God showing up in your story?

Chapter 13

What Story Do You Tell?

Being confident is recognizing we have a story we can tell with confidence.

I OFTEN HEAR women say, *I struggle to believe that God can use me because . . .*

> . . . *I was abused.*
>
> . . . *I am wounded.*
>
> . . . *I'm divorced.*
>
> . . . *I messed up.*
>
> . . . *I have Addison's, or cancer, or _____.*
>
> . . . *I feel broken.*

"How can I be confident when I have _____ in my life?"

The stories we want to tell to our world are those wonderful moments where we are brilliant and we perform with excellence. It's the version that shares our success and accomplishments. That's the story we want others to know.

But the story that people actually want to hear, the one that will make the greatest difference in our world, is the REAL story. That story has wonderful moments, yes. It does have tales of when we shine and thrive in our environment.

Yet it is also full of heartache, failure, and broken places. We have the scars to prove it. Those are the parts of our story that, even today, stir up the emotions within us and often bring tears to our eyes. We would rather not dig back into the whole story ourselves, let alone tell that story to someone else.

That's the story—the real story, the whole story—that will inspire our greatest service to the world.

Not because we have experienced the pain, but because our pain connects us to people who know that pain also, who have experienced loss similar to ours. Actually, it is more than that. Loss is a given. Sooner or later, we will all experience loss in our life.

While the pain is our connecting point, the real reason people are drawn to our story is because they want to hear how we got through it. How did we survive? How did we find our way?

That's why people listen to us when we say we know. We've been there. But more than that, it is because we have found our way through.

People ask: *"Can you point me to the hope?"*

Two quick stories:

1. The first was several years before my daughter died. I had the opportunity to hear a man speak by the name of Jerry Sittser. I was drawn to what Jerry might say because just three years earlier, he had been involved in an accident that took the lives of his wife, his mother, and his four-year-old daughter and left another child critically injured. He was being interviewed after having written a book called *A Grace Disguised*. I desperately wanted to know how this man could speak with such hope just three years after such tragic loss. [16]

   As it turns out, it was Jerry's book that helped lead me through the pain of my own grief of my daughter's death several years later. I knew he knew pain. I trusted him to serve as a guide as I walked through mine. (You can read more about Jerry's role in my grief journey in *Lovely Traces of Hope*.[1])

2. The second story was after Leisha died. The book *The Shack*[17] had just come out. People shared that it was about a man who had lost a daughter and how God was showing up in unusual ways for him. I really didn't want to read a story of someone else's pain in losing a child. I barely had the emotional capacity to deal with my own. But I read that book with ferocious desire to know if the man survived his loss; more accurately, I wanted to find out if that father saw God in his broken place and if God was enough.

I read these stories because I was desperate to know how they got through their pain. People tell me that they read my book *Lovely Traces of Hope*[1] to see if I really did find hope in the middle of my loss.

Every time I hear those comments, I recall the words one of my daughters spoke to me after she read the first rough draft of that book: *"Mom, I don't see any hope in your book!"*

Shortly after that, my friend Barbara and I chatted over a cup of coffee at Panera. *"The first twelve chapters you write as if you are standing among us naked and unashamed."* I almost blushed when Barb spoke, suddenly feeling very vulnerable.

Barb continued, *"But in the last part of the book, it is as if you put your clothes on. You become something else: a teacher, a coach. Someone who invests in the lives of others, but not being personal, going deep, or sharing intimately."*

I had quit being transparent in telling my story and tried to appear as if I had figured grief out, as if I now was the expert and could show you how to grieve. Don't get me wrong, I have learned a lot—not just about grief, but about living confidently in a world that throws devastation at us.

But the REAL story—the whole story that leaves me feeling quite vulnerable—is that I will always be a grieving mom. Just as I will always wrestle with feeling confident, even if I write a book on being *unstuck and confident.*

That's the truth of it.

For me to represent any other story leaves my reader, my listener, my friend feeling like either they must not be doing something right because they continue to struggle with the reality of loss, or they see through me and know I'm not being completely honest about my own journey.

In either case, they lose confidence in me. I lose my authenticity, my transparency, and my platform to speak into their journey.

Do We Have to Share THAT Story?

When we meet someone for the first time, what is the best way to get to know each other? We share our stories. We are not looking for dates and locations of their life. We want to know who they are, what matters to them, and how their life experiences have shaped who they are today.

We tell our stories and listen to the stories of others to be known and to know.

We will not tell all of our story to everyone, but when we do, it is important that we tell our real story for a variety of reasons.

We tell THAT story for ourselves:

As the storyteller,

- We begin to own the value of our own story. As we pull out of the day-to-day and look at the bigger picture of our life, we see how significant our stories have been.

- We notice how the seemingly random and separate stories connect. Rather than a long, straight timeline of events, our life is more like a slinky. An event that happens in the second grade suddenly connects to a county beauty pageant at age sixteen, which speaks volumes into my life at age forty-five.

- We affirm the lessons we have learned and our responses to those lessons that define us.

- We find our voice and recognize we are worthy of having a voice and being heard.

- We become:

  vulnerable, which makes us approachable.

  accountable, which keeps us honest and on-target with our goals.

- We get a clearer understanding of the difference we make.

  Our VALUES are clarified as we live out our significant moments.

  Our CIRCLE OF CONCERN is often born out of circumstances we experience.

  The NEEDS we see around us are often prompted by needs we have had ourselves.

  The PEOPLE WE CHAMPION most often resemble someone we have seen in our own mirrors.

- We help others, which enables us to turn a very dark and difficult part of our life into something that is actually positive and meaningful.

It has always been my prayer that I would be able to learn from my story and share what I learn with others. After Leisha died I often said, *"If I have to hurt this bad, it better be of help to someone else."*

That's the story that we must listen to ourselves. That's the story we must tell. Great stories involve both the beauty and the pain, the success and failure, the thrill of the victories and the messy middles. Nobody can tell your story better than you.

We also tell THAT story for others:

> *People want to hear the story of your trials, tribulations, and challenges.*
>
> —Janet Murray (Tribe Writers Conference 2019)

Why is that? Because until we hear someone's story that mirrors our own in some way, we feel like we are the only ones dealing with a loss, or dilemma, or painful relationship.

We tell our story to . . .

- Build trust with others. They need to know we get it and we've been there. We understand the issues they are wrestling with.

- Help them know they are not alone.

- Give permission to others be real about their story as we choose to be vulnerable with ours.

- Connect relationships, forming bonds that strengthen and support one another.

- Give Hope! Point to hope! If we can do it, maybe they can too.

- Share what we've learned, the steps we took, the books we read, and the people who helped us along the way.

Often people are looking for the "how-to's" before they look for the deep inner work that they will need to do. But we can help them see both are needed to move forward.

Telling the REAL stories, the truth, can feel dangerous, especially when we are right in the middle of sorting out the emotions, the relationships, and the pain for ourselves. The last thing we want to do in those times is open up about what is happening in us. The fear of judgment or expectations from others is too great.

Two things to consider:

1. Telling ONE TRUSTED friend, coach, or counselor could be just what you need to help begin making sense of the chaos. But note: I said TRUSTED. Someone who can see you in the mess of it all and still appreciate the journey you are on.

2. Often, we do not understand the stories as we are living them. Life is lived moving forward but best understood looking backward. Allow yourself some time and space to embrace some of those moments for yourself before you put it out there.

You may not be ready to tell your story. Please hear me when I say that is ok! But remember, our stories are good for us and for the people we live and work with.

Who is a trusted friend you could share part of your story with?

TAKEAWAYS:

Use the next few moments to write down your insights from PART THREE. You may want to jot down some thoughts about your story—the Red Sea story that changed how you view much of life.

BUDDY CHECK-IN:

This is a good time to touch base with your buddy. By now you have learned a great deal about each other. I challenge you both to share one more part of your story with one another. As you speak the words out loud, often you can see more clearly what the story has to say to you, and to others in your world.

Part Four

How Do You Express

How You Feel?

It's time to move on. We started this journey to confidence in Chapter 5 with a formula.

Honesty + Remembering = Intimacy, which leads to confidence

In Part Two, you identified that being confident starts with HONESTY about what's real about yourself:

- Being able to see things as they really are.
- Seeing yourself for who you truly are, recognizing you have been CHOSEN by God to be who you are in the body of Christ.

In Part Three, you considered how being confident means you are HONEST about your stories:

- Telling the truth about your story.
- Learning to listen to your story.
- Learning the lessons from your past
- Noticing God in your story.
- Recognizing you have a story you can tell with confidence

But the Psalmist, who gave us our formula in Psalm 77, also got honest about how he felt, specifically how he felt about God. There is significant value for us to consider how our emotions affect our ability to move forward, and even lead with confidence.

Our little caterpillar friend (in Part One) does not have the privilege of expressing verbally how she feels about anything. She simply responds to the life she has with the intuitive nature God has given her.

But our Creator gave to humans the gift of communication. Not just so we could communicate with one another but to afford us the opportunity to have conversations with him as well. We have the honor of not just sharing all that is good in our lives but also speaking how we feel about the good, the bad, and the ugly.

That includes how we feel about him, just as the Psalmist did in Psalm 77.

In Part Four, we will take an **honest look at the REAL emotions** we have.

How DO you feel?

Chapter 14

What Are Your Emotions Telling You?

AFTER A RATHER long video chat with a new client who had revealed painful parts of her story for the first time ever to another living soul, she blurted out, *"I know I shouldn't feel that way, but if I'm being honest, I have lived most of my life terrified that someone is going to find out who I really am. I have been nauseous just thinking about telling you the TRUTH of my story."*

After a moment of silence, I asked, *"How does that make you feel now that you have shared it with someone?"*

She paused, but only for a moment, *"Such relief! I have been carrying all of that baggage around with me for a very long time. I thought if I just kept it a secret, and no one knew, then I wouldn't have to deal with it. But it actually just got heavier and heavier the longer I tried to bury my past. It feels good to finally let it out and realize you are not judging me for the mess."*

I can't tell you how many times I have heard a woman say *"I know I shouldn't feel this way, but . . ."* or *"If people knew my whole story . . ."* What do those statements reveal? Uncertainty, doubt, fear, not only about being honest about our emotions, but also how they will be received by others.

We've been taught since we were young the "proper" way to deal with our emotions. If our family of origin was able to express openly and honestly how they felt, then we are more able to be open in our expression as well. If our family kept them private, hidden from the world and each other, we tend to do that now too. Much could be said about how, as a child, we learned to express ourselves, whether in our childhood home or at school, whether from family or other people in our life. I invite you to consider what your learned behaviors have been when it comes to how you express your emotions.

Who says you shouldn't feel the way you feel?

For whatever reason, this is how you feel. You don't always know why or where it came from, but before you can address those questions, you must be honest about what you are truly feeling.

Most of the time when I ask a woman to name her emotions, she is quick to respond with an accurate word: sad, angry, disappointed, ticked off, confused, peaceful, etc. But sometimes she says *"frustrated"* when she is down-right angry. Or she admits to feeling *"encouraged"* by something she has accomplished when she is very proud.

Or, as is the case with grief, her many emotions have become a tangled web of chaos within her. It takes a great deal of effort to separate them to allow her to identify what she is really feeling.

Emotions are a tricky thing.

One minute we can be really confident. I mean sexxy confident with the feeling of boldness and daring. We are willing to take significant next steps with a tremendous sense of confidence from the inside out. We FEEL confident.

Then something happens. We talk to someone. They say something odd or look at us the wrong way. Someone gets invited and we don't. What's that all about? Our thoughts go askew. *"I thought we were friends. Don't they like me? What did I do wrong?"*

Suddenly, we are in a puddle of doubt.

I know that is a bit dramatic. Usually it doesn't last very long and we regroup. But it lasts long enough to take our FEELINGS about how confident we are and dash them in the mud.

What do we do with our fickle emotions?

Making decisions based on emotions is not a good idea because they are prone to change without a moment's notice. I know people who feel strongly that we can't trust our emotions... and, therefore, we need to disregard our emotions and embrace logic.

But we need to really think about that. In his book, *Emotions: Can You Trust Them?* [18], well-known author and psychologist James Dobson writes, *"Emotions have a definite place in human affairs, but when forced to stand alone, feelings usually reveal themselves to be unreliable and ephemeral* (lasting for a short time) *and a bit foolish. On the other hand, it would be a mistake to minimize the impact of emotions on human behavior."* (Introduction p. 7)

Consider that our emotions are God-given. They are part of the design used to create us—part of our S.H.A.P.E. To disregard or not pay attention to them is to not be honestly assessing who we truly are.

Emotions play an important role in allowing us to experience the fullness of life. Some emotions invite to us celebrate goodness, hope, and delight. In those moments, we experience a great deal of the joy of life.

But there are also emotions we don't want to experience: sadness, disappointment, rejection, loneliness, and desperation. We don't want to feel those things. But in reality, that is also part of life.

Embracing both the good and the bad, the happy and the sad are all part of our understanding of the fullness and richness of life. Truly experiencing life is living in the tension between the two. That is life filled with emotion.

Our culture, upbringing, and relationships have instructed us in layers as to how we should handle our emotions.

Business professionals tell me that there is no room for emotions in the workplace. Emotions get in the way of getting things done, so we circumvent the emotion for the sake of the job.

Many women tell me that they can't share how they really feel about their situation because they "shouldn't feel this way, so . . . "!

We've all experienced moments when to speak truly of our emotions unleashes a word storm of confused, bitter, angry emotions of others. We choose not to go there.

But what happens when we shut down emotions at work? We are forced to work in an environment where our reality is squelched along with our creativity, freedom, and enjoyment.

What happens when we deny our true feelings? What happens when we stuff our emotions in hopes that we don't have to tell the truth about who we are and how we feel? We are compelled to hide the REAL about us. We become small and alone.

Our silence blinds us. We are unaware that there is a person in our life that longs to speak the REAL, but they also hide in fear, just as we do.

What happens in our families when we don't share how we feel in order to keep peace at the family dinner or holiday celebration? We become more and more distant from one another, never really knowing each other or the things that make our hearts beat or break.

WHAT IF we embraced the WHOLE of our emotions and experienced ALL of life—the polished and the messy, the beautiful and the ugly, the professional and the personal.

Counselor and author Holley Gerth writes:

> *Emotions are a big part of what makes you amazing. They allow you to respond to life in deeply personal ways. They connect you with others. They reflect your awesome Maker.*
>
> *Research has shown that there are six universal emotions: anger, fear, disgust, amusement, sadness, and surprise. How we display those emotions shows up in facial expressions that are recognizable in even the most remote parts of the world. Women . . . could walk through any door in any country and their feelings would be clear to those around them. Isn't that incredible? Our emotions display our hearts—our beautiful, broken, blessed, glorious hearts.*[6]

Do You Know What Your Emotions Are?

If you have read/worked through this book as it is written, Part Two helped you take a good, hard look at what your reality really is. If you started at the back or are skipping around, you might want to look at Part Two before you go further in this chapter.

Start by observing your perspective of your reality, and then, continuing to be honest, reflect on how you feel about who you are and the life you are living.

In this portion of the book, you are working to be honest in a constructive way—not just rehearsing all the things you like or don't like about your life, but being honest about the emotions tied to your experiences.

So . . . how do you FEEL about your life?

If you could use ONE WORD to describe the EMOTION you feel about your REAL life right now, what might that word be?

When I have asked women this question, some of the honest answers I have received are . . .

Unnoticed	Invisible
Unappreciated	Under-valued
*Lonely	Spent
*Exhausted	*Afraid
Limited	Uncertain
*Discontent	*Unconfident
*Blessed	Daunting
*Hopeful	*Nostalgic
*Determined	*Challenged
Transformed	*Unsettled
*Content	*Tired
Encouraged	*Stressed
Disheartened	*Hurt

Which words resonate with you?

Now take a second look at these words. Some of them are not actually emotions. Emotions are internal (*words marked with an asterisk). They depict how we feel within ourselves. But many of the words above are related to thoughts that form from external evaluations or judgments of others.

When we say we feel unnoticed or invisible, we observe that the people around us do not see us. That is an external evaluation of how things seem to be. The emotion comes when we identify how we feel about that.

When we identify our emotions within ourselves, we clarify what *we observe, feel, or need rather than diagnosing and evaluating the actions of others.*

That's when we can

- deal with the emotions and express them appropriately.

- communicate them effectively to others.

- hear real emotions of others and, therefore, care appropriately.

- address the feelings we have toward others that are part of creating our scenarios.

Take a few moments to just get in touch with the emotions you are currently feeling. What do you observe? What do you feel? What do you need?

NOTE: I have included a *FEELINGS WHEEL (with permission of the author)* in the workbook to help you identify the emotions you are experiencing. It is a great start in understanding what you may be feeling.

BUDDY CHECK-IN:

This can be an interesting exercise with your girlfriend. Share how your emotions are similar or different from each other. Seek to understand what you hear from one another.

Chapter 15

Why Do You Feel the Way You Do?

I HAVE BEEN fascinated by this question for a while now. There are moments in my life when something will happen that doesn't seem like such a big deal, yet the intensity of my emotion is *"over the top."* It doesn't matter if they are positive or negative reactions.

While I am not an expert in the "why," I am learning a great deal because of my work in this area and also of my own health journey. I met with a new doctor who specializes in how our brain works and affects our health. One of his questions to me was *"Is there anything that seems to keep coming up in your thoughts, something you replay over and over again?"*

"You mean like a song you can't get out of your head, or a conversation you keep rehearsing after it has happened?" I asked. The doctor nodded yes. I named a few things and then said, *"Well, I can replay the day my daughter died in vivid detail and feel the emotions of that day in the snap of a finger."*

"That's it!" he replied as he looked over at his associate. I was curious. The conversation that followed allowed me to gain a better understanding of the amazing way our brains are wired.

From the time we are young, we develop certain learned behaviors or responses to specific events, words, or relationships. The doctor called it *plasticity,* where triggers create pathways to learned behaviors.

He asked me to imagine that in my brain is a neighborhood. On one side is the development where families with school-age children live. On the other side is the school. In between the two is a park with a grassy field that the children walk across every day during the school year. By the end of the term, there is a well-worn path from the development to the school, leaving very little grass to grow there.

That path is much like the pathways our brains naturally make all the time. When certain things happen or we think certain thoughts, our mind takes the path it has most grown accustomed to traveling, the path of least resistance.

The day of my daughter's accident triggered a response of shock and grief. Each time I replayed the events of that day, the emotions became more deeply rooted. My responses were more intense to the point that my body's physical reaction became extreme.

The same is true every time I heard the words, or something similar to, *"not good enough."* My response as a second-grader was to throw up my hands and walk away. Over and over, my natural response to those words was the same. I threw up my hands and walked away from similar situations with greater emotion each time.

Being honest about our S.H.A.P.E. and our story is important. It allows us to understand how our emotions and responses from the past are influencing the behaviors, attitudes, and decisions regarding our future.

The good news is that we can create new pathways, new responses to the events or messages that trigger us.

Go back to that neighborhood in your brain. During the summer break, the pathway that leads from the housing development to the school starts to grow over. The kids don't walk there every day, and the grass has a chance to grow again.

That is what we want to do with some of our brain's pathways. We quit using the old paths to behaviors we don't want and allow the grass to "grow over" while we create new paths to new responses that are better for us.

Often we try to just tell ourselves a new truth we want for our lives. We use affirmations in an effort to help us create new beliefs. But if we don't believe what we are saying, it feels like we are trying to *force* something to happen. What we really need to address are the triggers that keep holding us back. Lies we believe. Responses we have to traumatic events.

When we decide to replace the lies with truth, we start that process of creating new pathways in our brain. There is no easy button. It takes intentional effort, perseverance, and time—lots of time. But it is possible and, in the long run, life-changing.

When you notice that your emotions are particularly strong or intense, try to identify the trigger: a message, a traumatic event, a tone of voice, etc.

You might want to trace back in your life map and see when other similar messages or events occurred. As you do, ask yourself these questions:

- What seems to "trigger" me?
- What message do I hear whenever this trigger occurs?
- What has been my response to those triggers in the past?

It may take some time for the recurring patterns to emerge, but trust me, making the effort to identify these markers can save a great deal of energy and pain as you break free from the pathways that lead you to destinations you do not want.

Remember in Chapter 7 when we discussed the passage from Romans 12? Verse 2 says *be inwardly transformed by the Holy Spirit through a total reformation of how you think. This will empower you to discern God's will as you live a beautiful life, satisfying and perfect in his eyes.*

Our strong emotions are invitations to transform how we think. It is that transformation that allows us to see what God's will is for us; to envision the life he has for us.

A simple way to address the recurring message is to . . .

- NAME the message you hear. Identify if this is in fact a lie or what part might be truth.

- CLAIM the truth God believes about you. This may mean you need to take some time to study God's word to see what he has to say.

Dana Gresh, founder of *Secret Keeper Girls,* shares that *"not good enough"* was her message also. In a college chapel message entitled "How To Overcome the Lie I'm Not Good Enough,"[19] Dana lets us in on the work she has done to create new thought patterns. (I've provided a link to her video message in the workbook.)

Dana claimed Ephesians 2:10. *We are his workmanship, created in Christ Jesus for good works which God prepared beforehand so that we could walk in them.*

The new pathway, or new truth, she created and spoke often to herself was

> *You are the fullest expression of God's heart
> in the form of a masterpiece.*

Read that statement again!

> You, my dear woman,
>> are the fullest expression
>>> of God's heart (imagine that)
>>>> in the form of a masterpiece.

WOW!

She summed it up by saying, *"Stop remembering all your sins and failures when you need to be remembering your Creator and the good works he has called you to do."*

Yes, that becomes our affirmation, but it is born out of our honest "right thinking" (as we discussed earlier from Romans 12). Right thinking about ourselves, our stories, and the messages we have heard. It allows us to embrace the truth about ourselves and how we really feel about that.

No, it is not easy. Once we have NAMED the lie, and CLAIMED the truth, then we must do the hard work of continuing to claim that promise even when our emotions may be trying to tell us otherwise.

And they will! They are familiar with the old pathway. It will take a while for them to take the new route.

I invite you right now to go to your workbook and identify which emotions are creating pathways you need to let grow over and where you want to Name & Claim a new pathway to a better outcome.

Emotions Act As Pointers

We've already stated that emotions are not always reliable, but we have also said that they are God-given and, therefore, must be important.

Remember in Chapter 11 when we looked at Mark 1:15, *"The time has come. The Kingdom of God is near."*

We identified the word TIME here as *kairos, not chronos,* which is our chronological, sequential word for time we use most often. *KAIROS* are those moments when heaven touches earth and the portal between the two worlds opens to allow our Creator God to break through and touch the heart of his beloved creation.

No matter the kind of moment it is, good or bad, happy or sad, long or short, when a *kairos* moment happens, God is close by! His kingdom is within reach as the margin between the two worlds gets thinner.

I bring this word up again because our emotions are not only simply identifying pathways in our brains, but they also serve as pointers for us, signaling a *kairos,* or an invitation from our Creator God to pay close attention.

Emotions make us aware that some part of our experience is connecting with the core of our design, the S.H.A.P.E. God has given us. When that happens, there is something about the moment that is significant and tied into who we are and what we were made to be and do.

We need to listen to those moments. Our emotions capture our attention and invite us to **STOP** to notice what is taking place.

It can be a response to a beautiful sunset after rain, or one of the defining moments we remember vividly.

But no matter what, we are stirred deeply by our emotions for a reason.

What are those moments in your story? If you worked through Chapters 9–13, you probably already know what some of yours are.

Take some time to identify the emotions that are attached to each one of those significant events. What was your response to your emotions? What pathways were created in your brain?

NOTICE what's really going on in the moment.

- How do you feel about the experience?
- How do you RESPOND to that experience?

What are your emotions pointing you to?

- Are they marking recurring patterns related to specific triggers?
- Are they signaling God-breaking-into-your-world *kairos* moments?

Spend some time in the workbook now and ask yourself the questions.

Chapter 16

So How Do You Feel About . . .?

Your S.H.A.P.E.?

REMEMBER S.H.A.P.E. STANDS for Spiritual gifts, Heart, Abilities, Personality, and Experiences.

I was a young wife of a seminary student sharing a few quiet moments with my pastor's wife, who I admired a great deal. Somewhere in our conversation she said to me, *"I wish I had your gifts. Aren't pastors' wives supposed to be able to play piano and plan big events for their church family? I'm just a quiet woman who loves the Bible and being behind the scenes."*

I was taken back. Yes, I did love to plan events and could play the piano, but not like my Momma. She had been my role model of a pastor's wife, and yes, I guess those things came quite naturally to me as well.

But the things I loved about this woman sitting next to me were all the things she was great at that I wasn't. She loved to facilitate women as they studied scripture and often invited members of our church for a quiet meal or would take a meal to people in need of support. I struggled to do any of that.

I spoke with another woman over a salad at Panera. *"I wish I was gentler and more soft-spoken,"* she said. *"I open my mouth and sometimes end up making a scene. I don't want that kind of attention."* I was shocked. It was her ability to speak up and create a scene that had just united a group of women together to make a real difference in her child's school.

I could share numerous other stories of similar conversations with women, including the woman reflected in my own mirror. We may be women who recognize who we are, but we don't always like what we see. I hear the message, *"I feel like I should be something or someone else."*

Why? Sometimes we may be comparing ourselves to other women. She may be the "scary" woman we have spoken about before. But she may also be our role model or hero in our life. We see values and qualities in her that we really do want to emulate, which may or may not be aligned to who we are.

Or perhaps we are measuring ourselves against the image that our culture markets to us. We don't have to look far to see a portrayal of how a confident woman should look. We feel like we need to work a certain kind of job to be successful. Or we should be a stay-at-home mom to be a good parent. No matter what choice we make, we feel like we are not measuring up.

That's what happens on a good day. Then life happens—the unexpected event like a health scare, or a car needing repair, or a new boss who wants to change everything. Our insecurity rises and gives way to fear. We begin to doubt. We think, *I should be able to do this. I should be able to make these changes and handle these things if I am a mature, confident, successful woman.*

But in reality, anytime we face something new, it will be a challenge for us. We have to learn new skills and new ways of doing things. And of course, if it is an unplanned event—good or bad—we are going to feel insecure. And yes, that may make us feel very much afraid. But that doesn't mean we must throw up our hands in fear and begin to recite all the old messages of self-doubt or inadequacy.

What if, instead . . . we reach out and embrace what is real, who we really are, and how we really live and feel right now? What if, instead of resenting or judging ourselves, we find a way to do it with contentment, gratitude, a generous spirit, and a compassionate heart?

Take a moment to review the insights you have had about your S.H.A.P.E. in Chapters 6, 7, and 8. See if you can name how you really feel about who you really are.

Experiences (Your Story)

How do you feel about the STORY you have lived?

I often work with women who wish they had a different story. Most of us have a sentence, a paragraph, or whole chapters of our story that we wish weren't true or at least could be rewritten. You have probably identified some of those defining moments as you were working to get honest in Chapters 9–13.

What do we do when we struggle with parts of our story? How do we address the feelings that are wrapped around those moments?

How do we recognize the message or lesson in the middle of those painful places, in those spots that leave scars? Are we able to acknowledge that these are not just random circumstances in our lives, that God uses it all to connect to us? He doesn't waste anything.

What are the events in your life that have left scars?

I feel deeply the scar that is left from my daughter's death. In the snap of a finger, I can be back in the intensity of emotions that I felt early in my grief. I didn't feel much in those first few days after she died. We were surrounded by people she loved, people that loved us. I was still numb to what had happened. But the days and weeks after everyone left were horrific. The darkness of the grief became overwhelming. The *chaotic cacophony* of emotions felt like it ripped my heart open day after day.

Some days we celebrate, we smile, or we laugh at some memory that brings joy to our hearts. Some days we are deeply grieving, angry, and fearful. And some days this happen seconds apart from each other.

Look at those defining moments, listen to how you felt in those moments.

They are part of what makes you *YOU*, with the passion that makes your heart beat and your heart break for the needs that you see.

The brokenness in my life has sometimes made it difficult for me to believe I could ever be amazing." God whispered to my soul, "You think you have to take what's broken and make it perfect in order to be used by me. But I think in a completely different way. I took what was perfect, my Son, and made him broken so that you could be whole. And because you belong to him, your brokenness can bring healing to others too.

— Holley Gerth [6]

Roles

Before we move on, look at your roles that you identified in Chapter 8. How do you feel about the roles you play in your current circumstances?

Too often, we focus on the problems in our reality. We feel stuck, forced to be the chauffeur for our kid, or cookie maker for the bake sale, or the caregiver for a parent, or the finisher for that project at work. Maybe all the above at the same time.

We may feel like we *have* to do these things for others. Yes, we love these people that we care for, but if we are honest, these tasks feel like small stuff. We feel that who we are at the moment doesn't really matter to the world.

What would that look like if we accepted the things we are doing now—things that feel small—and embraced them with a great love and a generous spirit?

We will talk more about roles later, but for now, just be honest about how you feel about each role. On a scale of 1–10, how would you say you are you doing in each role?

- Where do you see yourself thriving?
- Where do you need to let go of a role?
- Where do you need help?
- What are the attitudes, thoughts, and behaviors that you are expressing in those roles?

I encourage you to not skip this step. Even if you just spend a few minutes here, address how you feel about the things you are currently doing. This awareness is a valuable as you take your next steps with confidence.

> **BUDDY CHECK-IN:**
>
> *How is your buddy doing in the areas of S.H.A.P.E., Story, and Roles? It's time to check in and check on! You both have come a long way! Together!*

Chapter 17

How Do You Feel About God?

REMEMBER THE LESSON about confidence from the Psalmist of Psalm 77 (Chapter 5). He gets really honest about how he feels about God (Psalm 77:7-9).

The Psalmist writes . . .

> **7** Has the Lord rejected me forever?
>
> Will he never again be kind to me?
>
> **8** Is his unfailing love gone forever?
>
> Have his promises permanently failed?
>
> **9** Has God forgotten to be gracious?
>
> Has he slammed the door on his compassion?

How would you write this Psalm in your own words?

One woman simply wrote:

> *God, If I am I being honest about how I feel,*
>
> *when you didn't fix things like I think you should,*
>
> *I'd probably yell*
>
> *Where were you God?*
>
> *I don't think you were there.*
>
> *I didn't see you.*
>
> *Where are you now?*

Another woman cried out:

So . . . was I right?

You rejected me just like all the other people.

Why are you being such a bully?

Why didn't you show up when I needed you?

Why did you slam the door on me?

It is hard to know when and how GOD should show up. It is invaluable in the middle of all of your pain, your scars, to acknowledge how you honestly feel in your relationship with God. But it is also essential that you remain open to the fact that you may not be seeing him as he really is. God may not look like you think he should. He may not fit the box you have created for him.

And the thing is, he's ok with that! He wants you to see that he is there, but he knows the effect that the noise and chaos of life can have on you. He invites you to start where you are and be honest with yourself and with God about how you feel about him.

- How are you receiving from him?
- Where are you angry at him?
- When do you feel you are holding him at arm's length?
- When do you feel he is withholding from you?
- How do you sense his generosity in this small or insignificant place?
- Do you believe he is who he says he is?
- What difference does your answer make in your relationship with him?

Your view and your feelings about God—whether you consider yourself to be spiritual or not—become really important. They play a significant role in your confidence journey.

We all deal with this relationship differently.

I read of Emily G.'s struggle on Facebook one morning. I marveled at this young mom's response to the challenge she faces.

It has been a hard year. After being diagnosed with an incurable disease (MS) and trying to figure out the ups and downs of my new normal, I can be sure of one thing: theology matters . . . what you believe about God matters. I have clung to the truth that God is good, God is loving, and God is faithful. How do I know this? Because of Christmas. Because a Savior was born, bringing hope to a helpless world and joy to great sadness.

I spoke with my cousin Crystal about this because she and her husband, Doug, have found themselves in a life they could not have imagined. After having served for many years as the directors of a ranch camp in Alaska, Doug was experiencing tremendous headaches that affected his ability to work. After a great deal of travel and doctor visits, it was decided surgery was necessary to address a bleed in his brain that was putting pressure on the brain stem.

During the surgery, nerves had to be cut that left Doug not only dealing with the headaches but now unable to walk or talk as he did when he entered the hospital. After exhausting doctor visits and therapies, resources and strength, they finally resigned from their position at camp and built a new home suitable for Doug to maneuver in. They began living their new normal for their family.

When I asked Crystal how they were able to get through this, her response was *"It has got to be God shining through, because there is nothing in us that would give us the strength to do what we must do. Real grace is not shown in the good times or bad, but in the peace that comes in the middle of it all. We are only beginning to realize that God must be bigger than we ever knew him to be for us to survive, for this to be a good thing."*

I was struck by the power of her words to my own heart. I was humbled when she shared that these were her journal entries after reading *Lovely Traces of Hope[1]*. My journey with God had spoken into her journey with God and was now speaking back into mine.

She went on to share that while this has been the most difficult thing they have ever experienced, Doug has written two thirty-day devotional books over the last couple of years. It takes him a long time because he types one letter at a time. But she added, *"The books give eternal value to his day—an eternal perspective. We get a glimpse of the gift of the grace of God in the middle of all this."*

Wow! When we don't get it, don't understand, and can't fix it, God continues to show up powerfully with eternal value and the gift of grace.

My journey took a different turn. I lost confidence in God.

Do you know when I lost my confidence?

- It was not when I got sick,
- or when my daughter had an eating disorder,
- or the day I left my job,
- or even the day my daughter died.

It was the day I started to question whether God is or was the blessed controller of all things. Why would he let this happen? Why would a good God allow good people to hurt this much?

Can I trust you, God?

That wasn't the day my daughter died.

It was actually sixteen years earlier, part of my backstory from before she was born that significantly touched the moment of her death. My timeline came crashing together like a stretched out slinky with the two points suddenly snapping closed.

In August 1990, I confirmed I was pregnant with my third child. But I had also just found out that the newborn baby of a couple in our church was fighting for his life. This couple had already experienced much loss through miscarriage and stillbirth.

My heart was overwhelmed with conflicting emotions, unsure about having another child myself and concern for my friends. They thought they were finally having a healthy pregnancy. But suddenly, due to an error made in what was supposed to be a routine procedure, they were now fighting for their baby to survive.

I prayed, I begged, I pleaded with God to let their Baby Eric live. In my attempt to "fix" this, I frantically cried out, *"God, if a baby has to die—take mine. I have never experienced a loss of a child. But if only one of our babies can live, give Maureen her baby."*

But Baby Eric died!

My response? I was very angry. I thought my sacrificial offering was more than enough for God to see it was the perfect answer. But he didn't listen to me. I wrestled with my anger for months. If Maureen experienced this kind of pain over and over with nothing to say about it, no control, no choice, then God might allow something like that to happen to me too.

That was the day I lost confidence in God.

On New Year's Eve 1990, Ren was at a conference with some young people. I put my two oldest daughters to bed early, climbed into my own bed, and buried my head in my pillow to cry. I was exhausted from the emotions during the four months since Baby Eric's death.

As my tears began to subside, I took a deep breath, shook my head, and said, *"God, I don't get this. I don't understand why you allowed it. But I know you are God and I am not.* **I choose to trust you!** *I choose to believe you are doing something in this that I can't see now. I choose to put my confidence in you!"*

I slid under my covers and slept really well for the first time in weeks.

The next morning I rolled over, amazed at how refreshed I felt. Out of the corner of my eye, I saw the calendar that I hadn't changed since August, when Baby Eric died. It was the picture of a kangaroo with a joey in her pouch. The caption read,

"Do not neglect the gift that is in you!"

I heard the message loud and clear that day as I placed my hand on my growing belly. Leisha Danae Burrus was born April 28, 1991.

The Lord gave me the gift of my daughter for fifteen more years, and then she did die.

My response? At first, I said outwardly, *"God's got this."* But then, once again, the anger and fear intensified. I was yelling at God again.

The day after Leisha died, we found in the back of her most recent journal, a book she had started to write. She only wrote one chapter, but in it she tells this story of Baby Eric and how I struggled with his death. She told of that calendar page and the message that it gave me.

Then Leisha wrote, *"Mom knew that God was going to use her baby and even as hard as it was for her to accept it, she did. And I was born."* [1]

The slinky of my life came bouncing back together. 1991 came directly in contact with 2006. God had showed up then with a message on a calendar. Now I had another moment of decision. Am I going to trust God this time, or not? Will I put my confidence in a God that works differently than I have ever expected, who is bigger than I have ever needed?

It took me a while, but I chose to trust a second time. And once again, he met me intimately in core of this momma's heart.

One more layer of confidence wrestled and won!

How do you feel about God in your story?

> *You gain strength, courage, and confidence by every experience in which you really stop to look fear in the face. You are able to say to yourself, "I lived through this horror. I can take the next thing that comes along."*
>
> —Eleanor Roosevelt

TAKEAWAYS:

Use the next few moments to write down your insights from PART FOUR. Your insights will be helpful as you begin to sum up your findings in PART SIX.

BUDDY CHECK-IN:

Touch base with your girlfriend. How are you feeling about God in your story?

Part Five

What Questions Do You Ask

When You Are Stuck?

WHEW! WE'VE DONE a lot of hard, honest work in Parts Two though Four uncovering what is real and how we feel about it. We've already asked a lot of questions that have caused us to dig deep for answers.

The insights you have already gained may have you feeling like you are ready to move on, to make plans, and take action. Let's do this already! Right?

If that is how you feel, go for it! Identify those things that you are ready to do. Take advantage of the added confidence you feel because of what you have learned about yourself. Sometimes the awareness alone is enough to free us to move ahead. I'm cheering you on!

But in other areas of your life, the awareness may not be enough. No matter how clear you are about what you want, or how disciplined you are to make things happen, you still feel stuck.

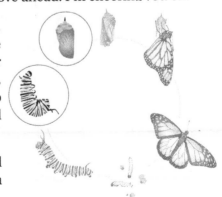

Asking the questions included in Part Five is similar to when the caterpillar turns herself into a pupa or chrysalis. She may look stuck—and feel stuck—like she isn't doing anything. When, in reality, she is entering a season of transformation and is being newly formed. She must embrace the hard things for the transformation to occur, for her body to change and grow and be made new. She is preparing to *be* what she was meant to be all along.

How many times do we *not* want to do that? The hard stuff comes up, and our first response is to throw up our hands and say *"Nope, I'm not doing that. I quit."*

The caterpillar instinctively knows that there is something MORE.

If you are experiencing a stuck place, rather than try to avoid, deny, or escape it, *what if* you embrace it? Accept that this is a place of transformation happening in the middle of the good and the bad. LIFE is best lived as you flow in and out of the stuck and grieving places to the free and confident opportunities.

That is where we are heading by following this process. For the

butterfly, she gets just ONE chance to go around in this circle. That is the entire lifespan for her. But we move through the circle many times throughout our life, maybe even daily. The process inspires a greater confidence to know and be who we were created to be.

Don't rush through this section. It is a significant aspect of your transformation.

Move on if you think you are ready. But make sure you mark this section because, most likely, you will be back at some point to dig a little deeper into the stuck places.

If you are ready to do that now, this will be a key place to spend some extra time. I promise, what you discover here will be worth every minute.

Chapter 18

Where Are You Stuck?

A FTER ALL THE work we have done in the previous sections, you might not feel like you are stuck anymore. After all, the new awareness about who you really are and what you are experiencing is often enough to free you from the STUCK that holds you back.

I am glad you have discovered what is remarkable about you.

But be alert that there are layers of stuck places in our lives. Finding freedom in one area may mean you need to release another area of stuck in order to move forward.

For instance, I have a pair of green rubber boots that I love. One day in early spring, I sat down to pull them off, but the moisture of the warm rain and the dampness on my skin made the inside of the boot stick to my calves with a Tupperware-tight seal. I would loosen the inside of my leg and move the boot down, but then I had to address the outside of my calf and do the same thing. One stuck place was impacted by another. I had to stop and laugh because as I worked on the outside of my leg, the inside would slip back into its original place. It took me ten minutes to finally peel that boot off my leg. And that was just one boot!

Yes, you may have released one area of stuck and now have great hope. Don't become disheartened if another area suddenly feels more stuck than usual. Just know you are taking steps forward, and that's where you want to go. For now, let's look at some areas where STUCK often shows up.

Are You Stuck in Your ROLES?

Go back to the ROLES you identified in Chapters 8 and 16. While these roles may give you a picture of what is real for now, they may not appropriately represent the life you want. In an effort to get each of your roles moving in the same direction, congruent with one another, take a closer look to see what changes you might need to make.

Since one of the goals of this book is to create confidence in life, let's look at eight significant areas that will help create balance and direction as you move forward. Each is important as you work to create the "bullseye," or destination, of your life.

How do your current roles line up with these categories?

Spiritual life

Family life

Professional life

Personal Development

Physical Health

Financial Health

Social Life

Community Involvement

Consider your life as a highway.

If each of the areas listed above are lanes of your life's highway, you would have eight lanes of interstate. The roles you play are the vehicles you drive in those lanes.

Each of your lanes need to lead you to the same destination. You choose where you want to go. If your roles are primarily focused on say, your professional life, it is as if you are only driving in one lane of your highway. Eventually you become so focused on only one area that you become a rather shallow person. If you try to involve yourself in all the lanes all the time, you become exhausted.

But the beauty of wisely managing each lane and the vehicles (roles) you drive is that this empowers you to have a life that is well-rounded and also worth living.

How goes the flow?

As you look at each individual lane, notice how they currently flowing. Sometimes you recognize that one lane is causing the traffic jams and affecting other lanes of your life. And that is important to pay attention to. It helps you get clear on what steps are needed to remove the obstacles in your way.

But sometimes you need to step back and see the big picture of your life's highway. So imagine that you have this special helicopter that takes you up high enough to see all the lanes of your highway at once.

I learned long ago that most people can only manage four to seven lanes of traffic (or roles) at a time. My mentors and the authors I have read often remind me that at different times in our lives, we need to switch up where our priorities are. We are, in a sense, changing lanes and focusing our attention on what matters most at any given time.

How many lanes do you have in your highway?

> What roles do you need to get rid of?
>
> What roles are missing that you want in your life? What can you do about these?
>
> What goals do you have for each lane?

The clearer you are on these goals, the more helpful it will be as you move through this exercise. If you are not sure about your end goal, write one sentence or word that describes what you see now. More clarity will come as you continue to process.

As crucial as it is for you to identify *where you are going,* it is equally important to figure out why you *aren't going.* What is holding you back from the very thing you want to accomplish?

To help you get a bigger picture of how one lane affects the other, ask yourself the following questions:

- On a scale of 1–10, how am I doing in each lane?
- What lanes/roles seem to be traveling freely?
- What lanes are stuck?
- How is each stuck lane impacting the lanes around it?

For instance, your professional lane is not producing the income you need to provide for your family. Therefore, your professional lane is impacting both financial goals and family needs.

Or your physical health is suffering. Certainly, that single lane impacts all the others. Making that one a priority has the power to greatly influence the rest of your highway.

- What stands out to you as you work through this?
- Where have you felt a stuck place release?
- Where are you moving forward with greater ease?

We will come back to this one more time as you pull everything together in Part 6. Thinking through your roles here will be helpful as you create your next steps in Chapters 27 and 28.

Are You Stuck in *WHAT IF?*

If you are paying attention as you read this book, you have noticed that I use these two words quite often when challenging an idea or presenting an alternative way of thinking about something.

But more often than not, *what if* comes up as a stuck place in my conversations with clients. Is this one familiar to you?

- What if I'm going to be like this forever?
- What if it's never going to get better?
- What if my marriage isn't going to change?
- What if I'm never going to have my health back?
- What if I'm never going to make any money?

What if . . . How do you use those two little words?

The words *what if* are powerful because they can be stuck words. They can be showing us what our fears are, what our guilt is, or where our shame is. Often, our *what if* questions show us what we're really feeling inside.

What if can *keep us* from seeing the possibilities.

But the beauty of *what if* (and what really makes them powerful) is that they can also *allow us* to see the possibilities.

- What if I try this and it *does* work?
- What if I *conquer* this particular challenge with writing? (That's one of mine.)
- What if I *accomplish* this goal I've had in my head for months or years?
- What if I could *lose* the next thirty pounds and *gain health*?

Imagine! *What if* we could do that?

What if I take one step, and then another step, and. . . You see where I'm going? Suddenly, those two little words *what if* become exponentially forward thinking, instead of a stuck place. *What if* becomes a catalyst for helping us see.

I recently watched a movie called *The Time Machine* (2002)[20]. Scientist and inventor Alexander Hartdegen is determined to prove that time travel is possible. His determination is turned to desperation by a personal tragedy when the woman of his dreams, the one relationship he was really sure of in life, was shot and killed in a freak accident. Now he is driven to want to change the past in an effort to save her.

What if I could? he asks.

Testing his theories with a time machine of his own invention, he goes back to that day, moments before she was killed. Time and again, he finds ways to change that moment of her death, only to have another scenario occur that still takes her life. He tries numerous attempts to change the outcome to no avail.

Finally, Hartdegen is hurtled 800,000 years into the future, where he discovers that mankind has divided into the hunter . . . and the hunted. The inventor's time machine is damaged in the landing. A young boy finds Hartdegen and takes him back to his village. While the scientist is healing, he discovers the people are terrified of something in the jungle.

At one point near the end of the story, he must confront the villain of that day in an attempt to rescue the boy and his people. The villain mocks the inventor for living life consumed by *what if.* The villain declares, *"You created the chaos that is now in the world as a result of your search."*

At this crucial moment when all seems lost, (spoiler alert) the inventor squares off and faces the villain, *"But you've forgotten one thing."* The villain pauses the destruction of the current world long enough to ask, *"What's that?"*

Hartdegen calmly says, *"What if?"* And with that, the inventor sees his way clear to conquer the villain, to take over the situation and save the current world he is in.

The professor had been trapped trying to create *what if for the past,* but couldn't change what he wanted to change. However, when he used *what if for the future,* it made all the difference.

How are you using *what if?*

For the past, which you can't change? Then *what if* will only reaffirm your fears.

What if nothing changes?

Or, are you using *what if* for the future? Asking *what if* I take this step in that direction? What's the possibility? *What if* I actually do what I think I can do?

Are you fearing the future? Or is *what if* drawing you to it, inviting you to envision the possibilities, the potential, the opportunities?

What if it did?

BUDDY CHECK-IN:

Share your insights with your buddy or in the Facebook group. We have already said that it is in sharing that we are all helped.

Chapter 19

What Are You Grieving?

LET'S CONTINUE TALKING STUCK places by considering what we might need to GRIEVE as we move forward. As I have worked with women, and worked through this myself, I have noticed layers of stuck places often related to

- Grieving WHAT ISN'T
- Wrestling with WHAT IS
- Struggling with WHAT HAS BEEN
- Fearing WHAT WILL BE

Let's take a longer look at what we may need to grieve yet. These are tender areas. You may not be ready to deal with some of these griefs, but I invite you to read on anyway. It will serve as a good prompt for when you are ready for this step.

Grieving What ISN'T

What are those losses in your life that leave you longing for something different than what you have now?

It may be the really hard things, even life-and-death situations, that change everything. These losses change your perspective and affect your ability to think and process. These things change you.

What isn't could pertain to any loss we have experienced . . .

- health
- job/career, or your ability to do that job
- relationships
- issues of aging
- financial loss
- . . . what would you add?

Your grief of *what isn't* could be a sadness over an expectation you had for this time of your life that has not happened. They could be times that keep you from having a vision because any plans you had for the future have been shelved. You are only surviving today. Vision becomes very moment by moment, breath by breath. That's all you can see. Even then, sometimes you can't see at all because the mud of grief is just so overwhelming.

I find often we don't really know how to grieve. We're not sure what that looks like. Perhaps we have seen someone else grieve their losses, and feel like we need to behave accordingly. But honestly, I can't tell you what it's going to look like for you. I only know what it looks like for me, and I only know that because each time I experience a new layer of loss, I have to go through another type of the grieving process. Even my own grief isn't always the same.

Stuck places don't always demand the same kind of grief. That's something that is unique to each person. Not only that, but grief is unique to each circumstance because our connection to that loss is different. My connection to the loss of my health was different than my emotions related to the loss of my job or the loss of my daughter. There are as many different levels of grief as there are different types of loss.

When you look back over your experiences that we discussed in Chapters 9–13, what events or relationships still bring up deep emotions in your heart?

What isn't that you desperately wish still was?
    (Examples: a job or a relationship you wish you still had, a loved one you wish was still living)

What isn't that you always wish could have been?
(Examples: a job you always dreamed of, a child you longed for but never had.)

What do you fear most about grieving for these things?
What do you think grief might look like for you?

Maybe something in the next few pages will prime your thinking in this regard. Let's keep going.

Wrestling with What IS

You've looked at *what isn't,* now consider how you are stuck in *what really is.*

Often when you are honestly embracing *what really is,* you find yourself stuck because you don't like *what is.* We have spoken about this before, but sometimes you're stuck wishing your current circumstance was very different than it is. You're stuck in what you think it should be or could be but isn't, and then you're back to grieving *what isn't* again.

You get caught in comparing your life to someone else's, and suddenly your life is not as good as theirs. Or you compare your life to your own expectations of what it should be. REAL is not as good as we hoped.

What IS are you wrestling with? When we can honestly acknowledge what's real, then we can deal with it. You already identified some of this in Chapters 9–13.

What IS that is causing you to be stuck?

- Owning who you really are?
- Embracing those messages you keep saying to yourself?
- A marriage you are struggling in?
- A job that sucks the life out of you?
- A child that tests you at every turn?
- What would you add?

Struggling with What HAS BEEN

Because you have lived your story, sometimes you think you know it. But when you take time to really listen to it, and identify those pieces and parts you call the high points, the hard times, the heroes, the un-heroes (or the villains), you see they have much to teach you.

We've talked about this before, but I want to be sure you take a look at how you might be stuck in *what has been* in your story—painful situations in your past that cause you to believe certain messages that are actually lies. There are images, senses, and triggers that you continue to connect with from days gone by. This goes back to the pathways in your brain that we discussed earlier.

When something happens today that ties in with *what has been,* we experience a reaction that is more intense than we think it should be. For example, my trigger, "I'm not good enough." Each time that came up, my response became more reactive—not because of the present moment, but because this moment now is tied to all the *what has been*s that have gone before.

As you worked through Chapters 9–13, you identified some of these defining moments in your life. Go back and identify the messages that came from your past experiences and continue to cause you to be stuck.

What has been in your life that keeps you stuck as you try to move forward?
What are the stuck places of *what has been* that you still need to grieve?

Okay. We've looked at *what isn't, what is,* and *what has been.* **Are you finding yourself stuck in any of these areas?**

When we are honest about our perception of loss and allow ourselves space to grieve those losses, we become freer within ourselves and with God. God already knows where we are hurting. He does. But he invites us to come to terms with these losses and find healing and freedom.

When we get stuck in one of those places, we can't move forward. Until we get honest, grieve, and experience freedom, we can't look ahead in a way that is authentic to who we are. We can't reach for what will be. Not really.

I know this all feels heavy, but stuck places are heavy, aren't they?

For me, I recall being stuck in the middle of the grief tunnel after our daughter died. The more I tried to move, the more grief just sucked me up and kept me from being able to breathe, let alone move.

Stuck sucks. Sorry if that offends you. But that's the truth. That's honest. Stuck is heavy. It's hard. It keeps us from the very life that we were made to live.

Where are you stuck?

Are you stuck with *what ISN'T*—grieving the losses?

Are you stuck in *what IS*—wrestling with what's real in your life?

Are you stuck in *what HAS BEEN*—struggling with past pain, lies we believe as truth, triggers that came from way back that are affecting us now?

OR are you stuck . . .

Fearing What WILL BE

If we aren't stuck in *what isn't, what is,* or *what has been,* perhaps we are stuck in being able to see *what will be.* We strive to find clarity for what the next step should be.

Often fear of the future is what keeps us from even trying to move forward. It is not always because we fear we might fail, though that is a common fear. No, it is more often fear that we will succeed and then what will we do.

So we don't do *anything.* Or we continue to sabotage our success and tell others *"I tried. It just didn't happen."*

For me, I struggle in my coaching practice, my business-building, and even writing this book. I do a great deal of legwork behind the scenes preparing what needs to be done to launch these things. But I often drop the ball in getting the word out because, well, if I do, what if people DON'T want to work with me, or read my books? Or . . . what if they *DO?*

What fears do you have of *what will be?* Are you willing to speak them out loud and begin to do something about them? I just spoke mine to you—and you are reading this book, which means I have found a way to overcome my fear.

What are your fears about the future?

Take a moment in the workbook to look at the grieving places where you might be STUCK. As we go through the upcoming chapters, you may find new places to add to your list. Right now we are just trying to identify what they are. Then invite the Lord to help you begin to process how to overcome them.

> **BUDDY CHECK-IN:**
>
> *Work with your buddy to talk through a stuck place you are struggling in. Then see if you can identify some ways to work your way through STUCK.*

Chapter 20

How Do You Respond?

The experience of loss does not have to be the defining moment in our

lives. Instead the defining moment can be our response to the loss.

It is not what happens to us that matters

so much as what happens in us.

— Jerry Sittser, *A Grace Disguised:*

How the Soul Grows Through Loss [16]

TYPICALLY, WHEN A client comes to me ready to take their next best step in life, or career, or relationship, we first talk through being HONEST ABOUT WHAT'S REAL (as in Parts One through Three) and ASKING the questions (as in Part Five). We don't always spend a lot of time here, but it is part of the process I use to see where we are.

Yet I believe that the topic of this chapter, actually the whole of Part Five, is perhaps the most impacting in my own life. This is where we take all our honesty about the REAL things and actually look at them for what we can learn.

Jerry Sittser reminds us in the quote above, that our *loss*—that stuff in our lives that usually leaves scars—doesn't have to be the defining moment of our life. Now it is true, we can let loss be that thing our whole world revolves around, be it the loss of a job, or a rejection from a spouse or child. Yes, it can threaten to define who we are.

But I read Jerry's book *A Grace Disguised* long before my daughter died, then again just weeks after her death. Jerry knows loss. Remember, his story involves losing his wife, his mother, and his four-year-old daughter in a tragic accident that also left a son in critical condition.

When he wrote that LOSS didn't have to define us, I wanted very much to believe him.

> *It is not what happens to us that matters*
>
> *so much as what happens in us.*
>
> — Jerry Sittser[16]

How would you finish this statement?

When _____ happened,

I felt _____,

I responded by _____.

Our RESPONSE is our defining moment.

Think back to our discussion about the recurring patterns or pathways (plasticity of our brains) that we discussed in Chapter 15. When we let our responses go unchecked, they become those common pathways our brains use like an *easy button* to solve problems for us.

Often it is a *pathway* that was learned in our childhood, or in a moment when tragedy struck. Neither time is prime for clear, mature thinking. But by constant use, the pathways become our preferred method of responding when we face similar situations.

That response may not be helping us.

When I asked a group of women to share how they typically respond when the hard stuff happens, here are a few things they shared.

- *Keep busy, or try new things to try to distract the pain.*

- *Turn up the volume—music, movies, phone or social media time to keep from thinking or hearing my own thoughts.*

- *Fill the void with "comfort"—other people, food, substances, tv, shopping, etc.*

- *Put on plastic smiles and deny what is true or how I really feel.*

- *Appear "strong" on the outside when I am crumbling on the inside.*

- *Put on masks and "play" like I'm ok, got my act together. I can look better than I think I am.*

- *Keep secrets—or hide truth.*

- *Blame others.*

- *Become intensely angry or fearful.*

- *Ask questions and seek answers, which leads into ASKing the questions we are asking now.*

That's quite a list. Which of these responses do you resonate with? Or do you have others you would like to add?

Jerry is saying that the defining moment in our life is NOT the event, but rather our response to that event. That would imply that we can do something about what defines us.

Often the event or circumstance is beyond our control. But we have a choice as to how we will RESPOND to it. Our response is the key variable that can change everything.

Consider this formula: **Event + Response = Outcome.**

Think about that for a moment!

Your responses to the circumstances in your life are creating the very outcome you are experiencing. Now hear me, I am NOT saying your behavior or attitudes CAUSE the losses in your life. Sometimes you have control in those situations, but often you do not. Please hear that.

BUT you do have the ability to choose the kind of response and, therefore, determine the outcome you get. How does that make you feel?

Consider how your behaviors and responses are affecting your confidence. Let's play out some scenarios based on the responses the women gave earlier.

What is the outcome when we . . .

Response	Reaction	Outcome
Keep busy / distracted	We may actually get a lot done. When we know we have to do a hard thing, we find all kinds of other things we could be doing instead.	We must keep running faster and faster for fear the real issues will catch up with us.
Fill our voids with 'comfort'	We might gain weight, or go in debt, or become addicted.	We always feel that empty place in our life.
Keep secrets / hide truth	We get creative at ways to skirt around the truth.	We constantly fear being found out.
Blame others	We might be able to feel relief personally—for a while	We fear we might actually be to blame— whether we are or not.
Put on smiles or masks	We feel protected behind the masks.	We feel more and more alone as we do.

How are you responding to the events in your life?

What are the recurring behaviors that are influencing how you move forward?

What's your response?

BUDDY CHECK-IN:

Talking through your responses may make you feel rather vulnerable, but I encourage you to have the conversation with this girlfriend you have trusted with your other STUFF. Handle each other's responses with care. Identifying them is one thing, but it may take some time to process how to deal with them. Be encouragers.

Chapter 21

Why Do We Masquerade?

MORE TIMES THAN I can count, women say to me, "*If people really knew me, or my story, or what I was really like, I am afraid they wouldn't like me. They wouldn't approve.*"

Is that it? Are we trying so hard to *be approved by others* that we are afraid to be honest about our own reality? Do we truly believe that others are so much better than we are that we stay insecure because of our certainty that we do not measure up? Are we so afraid that we will be found out as an imposter that we try to be something we are not—and actually become the imposter?

We can all get pretty good about putting on the masks and pretending we indeed have it all together. We can choose what we want others to see when they look at us. We can hide all the unsightly past or the pain of the present. We can masquerade around as if happiness exudes from us and our dreams all come true.

Could it be that we, ourselves, are afraid of what we will find if we even lift the mask a little, let alone take it off?

Pretending can be fun for a while. Who doesn't enjoy dressing up occasionally for a masquerade party? But masks can be fragile, breakable, suffocating. They are hard to keep on and hard to keep up! Creating the storyline you wish to portray to the world becomes a challenge because before long you forget the story you manufactured and get caught in the lie.

That prompted me to think of another time when people did that. It is a story about the Garden of Eden found in Genesis. (Words in **bold** are my emphasis.)

> **Gen 2: 25** Now the man and his wife were both **naked**, but they **felt no shame.**

> **Gen 3** The serpent was the shrewdest of all the wild animals the Lord God had made. One day he asked the woman, "**Did God really say** you must not eat the fruit from any of the trees in the garden?"

> **2** "Of course we may eat fruit from the trees in the garden," the woman replied. **3** "It's only the fruit from the tree in the middle of the garden that we are not allowed to eat. God said, 'You must not eat it or even touch it; if you do, you will die.'"

> **4** "**You won't die!**" the serpent replied to the woman. **5** "God knows that your eyes will be opened as soon as you eat it, and you will be like God, knowing both good and evil."

> **6** The woman was convinced. **She <u>saw</u>** that the tree was beautiful and its fruit looked delicious, and **she <u>wanted</u>** the wisdom it would give her. So **she <u>took</u>** some of the fruit and ate it. **Then she <u>gave</u>** some to her husband, who was with her, and he ate it, too. **7** At that moment their **eyes were opened**, and they **suddenly felt shame at their nakedness.** So they sewed fig leaves together to **cover themselves.**

> **8** When the cool evening breezes were blowing, the man and his wife heard the Lord God walking about in the garden. **So they hid** from the Lord God among the trees. **9** Then the Lord God called to the man, **"Where are you?"**

> **10** He replied, "I heard you walking in the garden, so **I hid. I was afraid** because **I was naked**."

> **11** "Who told you that you were naked?" the Lord God asked.

"Have you eaten from the tree whose fruit I commanded you not to eat?"

12 The man replied, "**It was the woman** you gave me who gave me the fruit, and I ate it."

13 Then the Lord God asked the woman, "What have you done?"

"**The serpent deceived me**," she replied. "That's why I ate it."

You know the rest of the story (If not, check out Genesis 3). There is much we could talk about, but my purpose here is to look at the *responses* in this passage.

In the first verse, the man and woman "were both naked, but they **felt no shame**." Naked is very real, very vulnerable. It's hard to hide anything when you are naked, right? But in the Garden, they had no reason to hide up to that point. God had created them, and they were free to respond without any fear or shame. Think of it.

But in Chapter 3 of Genesis, their authentic vulnerability and their confidence in God is brought into question by the *serpent*. "*Did God really say . . . ?*" or "*You won't die . . . !*"

Eve's response?
> She was convinced.
> She saw.
> She wanted.
> She took.
> She gave.

The outcome? Their eyes were opened.

> **They suddenly felt shame** at their nakedness, for the first time ever.

Their response? They covered themselves, they hid from God, and they blamed someone else.

We could go on to look at the conversation they had with their Creator at that point, but I encourage you to read more of the story for yourself.

I thought back to the losses I have experienced in my life. With each loss I mentioned, I did believe that God was the Blessed Controller of all things.

I also noticed that the *enemy* came in subtle form and began to cause me to question.

- Why would God let my daughter die?
- Why would a good God let people hurt like this?
- Has God forgotten to be kind?
- Where are you God?

Does that remind you of other questions we spoke of in Psalm 77, verses 7–9 (Chapter 17)? That's how the Psalmist really felt. That's how I really felt. This is being honest.

But even as we are honest, we need to consider the enemy is behind those thoughts, prompting us to lose confidence in the very God who created us in the first place. The God who gave us life, who redeemed that life and continues to pursue a personal relationship with us.

How did I respond? Often, I chose to *cover* myself. Maybe it was to protect myself, but sometimes it was to hide my flaws, or my doubts, or my broken places. I was ashamed of the scars that were left to prove I *"don't have it all together."*

Until I realized my *fig leaves* were more like *"burial clothes."* I was hiding, and therefore, not taking care of the wounds life had hurled at me. Now they were festering, decaying, dying. I had done such a good job of covering myself that I had created my own shroud— my burial clothes. Instead of healing, I was actually creating the outcome I was trying to avoid.

What's YOUR RESPONSE?

Are you hiding behind the *fig leaves,* covering up STUFF that doesn't measure up, hiding the flaws? Dressing for the part you wish you had instead of the role you were meant to play?

We PUT ON stuff—not to be modest but to hide, to cover places of weakness.

- Sometimes those are things that are just different from others.

- Sometimes we cover up what is real to create the illusion we want people to see.

- Sometimes we hide our scars that we are

    ashamed of,
    embarrassed by,
    afraid to share.

- Sometimes we put on masks so others won't see our ache, guilt, or shame.

- Sometimes the wounds have become dead places, and our coverings become burial clothes.

We try to escape the painful awareness that we have listened to the enemy or have doubted our Creator. We feel deep emotions for the outcome our response has produced.

We say "fine" when we are asked how we are doing, when everything in us wants to scream . . .

My marriage is miserable!

My kids are maddening!

My job sucks!

HOW DO YOU THINK I'M DOING?

What is heartbreaking is that when we try so hard to *cover up* and "look like" we have the good life, we actually manufacture the very things that keep us from it.

Oh, we have incredible masks, don't we? They are as beautiful as we can afford to make them. Such sweet masks. Those masks always have such a polished look. People put them on when they come to church, or to community events. It says through plastic smile, *"I'm okay. Yeah, everything's great. We're doing wonderful. How are you?"*

But at what cost?

We become people who say, *"If you really knew who I was, you wouldn't like me."* Inside, you know you are not who you are pretending to be, but you fear showing up as you really are. What if people hear the doubt in my heart, or uncover the choices I made that I am ashamed of, or reveal that I don't have a clue how to deal with all this STUFF.

Is that you?

How do you know people will not like the real you?

If you're not being real with them, you're probably not being real with yourself either. And if you are not being real, if you're not *grieving what isn't* or *what is*; if you're not embracing *what was*, or *what will be*, then you are not identifying who you really are either.

You paste on your plastic smile, dress up in your best look, and pretend all is well! You pretend you are already a butterfly when, in fact, you are still a caterpillar who has not found a place to form a chrysalis. Very quickly, you exhaust your reserves and find yourself running from one masquerade to another.

What if . . . instead of all that pretend . . . we live real?

What if we accept who we really are—good and bad, happy and sad, easy and hard?

What if we embrace the places of our stories that hurt us or that we are ashamed of?

What if we grab hold of those pain points we want to write out of our lives, and instead allow them to speak into the person we are today?

What if we truly celebrate our uniquenesses as being enough?

What if we recognize that these very broken places are what God wants to use to make a difference in our world?

What if you being real allows others to be real, which encourages ALL of us to be real together?

We smile when we can—and we cry when we need too.

We share it with others—not the whole world, but with those we dare to share with.

We allow them to share their STUFF with us.
And we smile with them.
And cry with them.

What if then?

Who are you really with the masks down and the fig leaves off?

You are a gift. Not just a gift to yourself, but a God-designed, God-given gift to the world. Your response frees you to authentically understand how you can live out what God wants you to do to make the difference he wants you to make.

That he made you to make.

That's when we are confident women!

> **BUDDY CHECK-IN:**
>
> *Are you still hiding, or putting on to cover parts of you that you are afraid to share with your world? What if . . . you did it anyway? See how you and your buddy and spur one another on to being who you really are in your world.*

Chapter 22

Where Are You Making Excuses?

WHILE WE ARE still looking at our responses, I think it is important to consider another response we often have.

In Chapter 2, I shared a story about a woman, a champion in my life by the name of Jenn. The three questions Jenn asked me on our very first meeting were...

Do you know your value?

Do you offer value to those in your world?

Are you getting paid what you are worth?

When I hemmed and hawed with my answers to those questions, the next thing she said to me was this:

> **"When you are done making excuses,
> you can get down to your business."**

Yep! That was the bottom line! I was making excuses about why I wasn't being successful or having the kind of influence I wanted to have.

Are you doing that? Making excuses instead of doing the things you really want to do?

Isn't that true of most of us when we don't know our value, when we don't realize who we are? I thought I did. I had spent a great deal of time and money going to workshops, reading, and researching personalities and strengths—seeking to understand and to help others understand who they were made to be and do.

Yet, there I was . . .

Struggling to see me, in a role that was actually not much different from the previous positions I held in my life. I had often struggled with my value—or the value I offered. Much of that was because I kept comparing myself to others. Or I tried to live up to what I imagined their expectations of me.

Now in my role as coach and entrepreneur, the lie I had believed as truth resounded loudly whenever I tried to take a step forward in my own business. *You are not good enough. Who would pay you to coach them?* I had started to believe that.

Instead of being honest and dealing with the issue of my insecurity, I made up lots of excuses for why my business wasn't working. I blamed *other people* who didn't see the value in paying a coach to help them move forward.

I spoke with Jenn most Wednesdays at noon in 2016 because she joined my *Power Hour* groups I hosted over the phone. Here she was—*my* coach—allowing me to be *her* coach. I was honored. These groups were designed to support women and hold them accountable as they accomplished their goals during a thirty-day challenge.

At the beginning of each five-week *Power Hour* series, the members would decide on the ONE GOAL that they wanted to accomplish during the next thirty days. Each week, we would declare the ONE ACTION that we would take that week to move us closer to our big goal. We would then hold each other accountable to those goals when we met the next week.

I got to listen to Jenn as she took her next big steps in life and business.

But what you may not remember about Jenn is that she had ALS: *amyotrophic lateral sclerosis.* In the United States, ALS is often called Lou Gehrig's disease, named after a Yankees baseball player who died of it in 1941.

When I met Jenn nearly three years earlier, she was still walking quite well, though with a cane. By the time of our *Power Hour* calls, she was confined to a wheelchair and dependent on her gracious husband, Dr. Bob, and others to care for her and the things important to her.

In one particular session, I challenged Jenn about the BIGness of her goal, especially in light of the limitations she was facing due to ALS. *"That's a lot to do in one week,"* I said. *"What if you break that down into more manageable, bite-sized pieces?"*

Her answer took our breath away.

"Kathy, while I have a mind to think it, and hands to do it, I must take on the BIG things."

Each one of us in the group went back to look at our goals—and the "excuses" we made as to why we couldn't do more. We each took a deep breath and made a decision to add some BIG to our vision and our commitment to it. If Jenn could do it, so could we!

How about you?

- What excuses are you making?
- What are those excuses keeping you from doing?
- What are you putting on hold until life is right?
- What are you hanging onto from your past that keeps you from moving forward?
- What keeps you from breaking that chain and "getting after it"—whatever *it* is!

What if we rise above the excuses, the blaming, the messages, the emotions—and just DO IT? What would that look like? How would that feel?

This isn't the end of Jenn's story. She will show up again before the book is through.

In the meantime,

- take a look at the questions above and get honest with yourself.
- Consider how your excuses are keeping you from taking your next best step forward—big or small.

What kind of response do you want to have in order to create the outcome you long for? Let's quit making excuses and get after it!

TAKEAWAY:

What is your takeaway from PART FIVE?

Take some time to ponder your excuses.

BUDDY CHECK-IN:

Have you been making excuses to each other in your effort to finish working through this book? Remember the commitment you made to yourself and each other to finish what you have started? Ok! Let's do this!

PART SIX

THE POWER OF A PIVOT

HONESTY is where we begin the journey to confidence.

We've been honest about a lot of things: our reality, our S.H.A.P.E., our stories, our feelings, our stuck places. Whew! That's a lot of honest.

But honesty alone can turn us into very raw, critical, and often bitter people who replay the same response to our STORY over and over, digging deeper ruts and crevices for us to get lost in.

Once we have been HONEST, what's next? How do we move forward to what we really want?

Do you remember our discussion in Chapter 5 where the Psalmist gave us a formula from Psalm 77?

Honesty + Remembering = Intimacy, which leads to confidence

After the Psalmist gets honest about what's real and how he feels about it in the first ten verses of the psalm, he then makes a PIVOT. In our formula, the pivot is a plus sign.

He makes a choice to turn from his honesty about the circumstances he finds himself in to . . . what?

Well, let's find out!

Chapter 23

A Pivot to Remember

THE PIVOT IN Psalm 77 is only two verses of the chapter, but these verses are a critical step in the outcome of this psalm. Let's look at them more closely.

Psalm 77:

> **11** But then I **RECALL** all you have done, O Lord;
>
> I **REMEMBER** your wonderful deeds of long ago.
>
> **12** They are constantly in my thoughts.
>
> I **MEDITATE** on your mighty works.

It appears that nothing has changed for Asaph, the psalm writer. His situation is exactly as it was in the early part of the chapter. Except that in these short verses, in a moment of crisis, he makes an intentional choice to **turn from** all that he has noticed in his reality and all the emotions that are welling up inside of him.

And he makes a three-step Pivot:

> I will recall.
> I will remember.
> I will meditate.

On what? On God. He chooses to remember God. And that makes all the difference.

In those moments that shake us to the core, when we come to an end of ourselves, we are invited to PIVOT. I might paraphrase it this way:

> *Ok, God! I don't see this as good. I don't see how this can be part of your plan for me. But you are God. I am not! I will consider all that you have done in the past—the history of the world past, but also in my past. I will turn from the circumstance I find myself in, and I will remember who you are and what you have done.*

The Passion Translation says it this way:

> Yet I could never forget all your miracles, my God,
>
> as I remember all your wonders of old.
>
> **12** I ponder all you've done, Lord, musing on all your miracles.
>
> **13** It's here in your presence, in your sanctuary,
>
> where I learn more of your ways.
>
> For holiness is revealed in everything you do.

In the middle of the chaos, we PIVOT to REMEMBER God.

I've been pondering the definition of this word *remember.* Here are a few definitions I have collected:

> to call to mind
>
> to think of again
>
> to bring back to mind by effort
>
> to recollect
>
> to recall
>
> to keep in the memory
>
> to be careful not to forget
>
> to remind
>
> to keep a person in mind with some feeling
>
> to keep a person in mind for a present *(such as remember the waiter with a tip)*
>
> to mention a person to another as sending regards *(remember me to your mother)*

Wow! There are many different aspects of remembering!

One definition that I noticed right away is the phrase *"bring back to mind BY EFFORT"*! It takes effort to remember, to call to mind. Once again, the Psalmist is inviting us to hard work! Yes, remembering is difficult because it stirs up emotions and generates energy that can be deeply inspirational or completely draining. It also takes a great deal of time.

But as we will soon be reminded, when we choose to PIVOT to remember, powerful things happen.

Notice this also: the definition describes remember as *to have in mind, or be able to bring to one's mind an awareness of (someone or something that one has seen, known, or experienced in the past).*

What we are actually doing is taking something from the past that is already in our mind and *RE*-minding ourselves of it,

> *RE*-turning to it by bringing it back into our thoughts.

> *RE*-connecting with someone or something in our past as in a memory.

Let's make that PIVOT and *RE*-member together.

What do we need to REMEMBER?

Too often we remember what we should forget and forget what we should remember. What are some things that might be important to recall or remember?

Scripture is full of things we are called to remember. Just do a search for the word in a reference guide like BibleGateway.com. But what was it the Psalmist tells us to remember?

> I will **remember** the deeds of the Lord;
> yes, I will **remember** your miracles of long ago.

Then in the next psalm, Asaph goes on to say,

Psalm 78:35:

> They **remember**ed that God was their Rock, that God Most High was their Redeemer.

We choose to REMEMBER Who God is.

In *The Gift of Being Yourself*[21], David Benner writes:

> *We do not find our true self by seeking it. Rather, we find it by seeking God. In finding God, we find our truest and deepest self. The anthropological (which means the study of man) question (Who am I?) and the theological (study of God) question (Who is God?) are fundamentally inseparable. It is by losing our self in God that we discover our true identity.*

Think about that! We choose to REMEMBER GOD because our confidence comes in knowing who God is, and therefore knowing more of who we are.

How do we do that?

In order to remember things about God, we must first know things about God. In order to recall what he has done, we need to pay attention to what he has done and is now doing.

His Word reminds us and teaches us of his character
and of his story (HIS STORY = history).

But our own story also teaches us of his character
and of his hand in our story (MY STORY = mystery).

That means we need to be alert. He may show up differently than we expect. Sometimes that is why we miss him—he's not like we think he will be.

Clients often say they have trouble remembering events from their own past. *"That was long ago. I don't really remember."* Here is what I suggest to them:

1. Invite God to help you remember the important things. Remembering is his idea after all. He has invited you to remember, and he will help you.

2. Then give yourself space in your life to let the memories surface. It's not your goal to remember everything, but if you *prime the pump* so to speak, the more significant, transformational memories will come flooding into your mind.

Other clients say *"I don't want to relive the past—I want to keep moving on."*

We don't always have to go back and relive the past. But as we already discussed in Chapters 9–13, we do need to go back to see how the messages from the past are affecting the behaviors, decisions, and attitudes of today.

Taking time to recognize what we remember about the past and how it might be keeping us from moving forward is invaluable. It plays a huge role in giving us the confidence to take our best next steps.

But more important is noticing— perhaps for the first time—where God's story is touching ours. There is nothing more powerful than to sit with a woman who sees where God's fingerprints are in her story, especially when all along she had wondered where he had been.

Throughout this book, I have used the illustration of our timeline being like a slinky. Imagine stretching out the slinky as far as you can without overstretching it. There can be quite a distance from one end to the other.

What happens when you let go of one end? The slinky claps together quickly, making the two ends very close to each other.

Our story is a slinky of sorts. In a heartbeat, an event from today can cause our story to come clapping together with a moment or message from years ago. Suddenly, who we are from our past touches who we are today. That is when we see not only God's fingerprints but his hand at work over and over again.

In his book *A Grace Disguised,* Jerry Sittser shares a story from his grief journey that has had a great impact on my own.

He spoke of a recurring daydream he had of a setting sun. He was frantically trying to lasso the sun and keep it from going down in the west. But every day, no matter how hard he tried, the sun beat him to the horizon and was gone. He was left standing in the twilight, knowing he would soon be overtaken by the darkness.

He dared to share his dream with his sister. Her response to Jerry cut me to the core. *What if you let go of the rope?* she said. *The quickest way for anyone to reach the sun and the light of day is to not run west, chasing after the setting sun, but to head east, plunging into the darkness until one comes to the sunrise."[16]*

Suddenly, with those words, Jerry's story touched mine. I slammed the book closed and threw it into the corner of my room. NO, this was too hard. I wouldn't go there. Jerry's dream took me back to the night and the place my daughter died—one and a half miles EAST of my home.

It took weeks before I picked the book back up, but I sensed that Jerry's sister might be right. As I felt my fear begin to settle down, I heard God say to me,

"Kathy, come meet me at that corner, just as you are—broken, mad, afraid. Come as you really are. I will be there with you."

I walked down my long driveway and down the mile and a half of country road that Leisha had walked the night she died.

And God met me there. Not just in the moment, but as the God who was, and is, and always will be. Every part of who he is touched every part of me.

All of life's slinky clapped together. The portal between heaven and earth opened, and my Creator, Father, God touched the heart of this created child, his beloved.

BUDDY CHECK-IN:

Look back over your stories. Where do you see your slinky suddenly bringing your past together with your present? Or the bigger picture of the God story as it speaks into the story of you?

Chapter 24

What DO You Want?

DO YOU REMEMBER the last time you were asked that question, let alone answered it? Oh, I know in the middle of the messiness of life, sometimes we throw the question out there. It probably comes out more like, *"Why do I always have to do what everybody else wants me to do? Why can't I have what I want?"*

When a mentor recently asked me this question, I replied, *I want a lot of things.*

> I want my shower to be fixed in the master bedroom.
> I want the windshield in my car to be repaired.
> I want our debt to be paid off.
> I want our family to be together again.

Then I realized most of those answers were related to things I just need to schedule on my calendar. But the question was asked to help me identify what I want for my future. Once again, I found myself hesitating to answer.

There were times in my past that I was pretty clear on what I wanted. But in the messiness of health issues and leaving jobs, I lost sight of some of that.

I was just starting to dream a big dream in 2006 when Leisha died. Then it was all I could do just to breathe and survive, let alone have any sense that there was a future to dream about. My head knew there must be something more, but my heart and body, at times, felt only death.

It took me over ten years to begin to dream again. During those years, I was consumed with what I HAD to do, not what I wanted to do or what I dreamed of doing. But over time, I remembered how to dream again. It became possible again to ask, *what do I want?*

What do YOU want?

> *Before you can answer the question "What am I going to do?",*
> *you've got to first ask, "What do I want?" That shift in focus will*
> *change completely how you respond in your life.*
>
> — Tony Robbins

As I dug for my answers, they felt a bit stymied. Honestly, my immediate thought was I wanted what SHE has. (You know, that woman who I have been comparing myself to.) That is until I imagined myself in HER shoes and started shaking in my boots. No, I do not want what she has after all. Even if I could get it, I really don't want to experience all she had to go through to make it happen. Even if I could get where she is, I would be miserable. It would be completely out of character for who I am and what I love to do.

But somewhere along the line, I began to believe that I needed to be realistic, to *stay inside the lines* and do what was practical instead of bringing my own dreams to reality. I learned that being realistic and being honest about what is real are two different things.

Being honest allows us to find a starting point from which we begin building our dreams. Being realistic is often more about the beliefs that stop us from being able to act on those dreams.

Zig Ziglar used the term *wandering generalities* to talk about people who complain about never having opportunities in life but can't tell you what they want.

Author and coach Dan Miller describes these people as *"not happy where they are but can't tell you where they want to be."* People who succeed *"approach every situation with the enthusiasm, confidence, and boldness that comes only from having a clear plan of action and the anticipation of a positive outcome."* [4]

They know what they want and they go for it.

I quit trying to come up with the perfect answers and asked the Lord to show me what I truly want for my life. After all, he created me to be me! He invited me to take an honest look at what I desire for my life, and align my actions with my values.

WHAT DO I WANT?

Hmm? I . . . want . . . MORE!

I want to make MORE of a difference in my world—just like most women I work with long to do. For me that means being able to . . .

- make connections with people where and when it matters.
- generate income that not only pays my bills but also provides for my dreams and generosity to others.
- be of service to my world.

I want to . . .

- inspire people to LIVE REAL.
- empower them to make their own authentic difference.

I want to be a . . .

- great wife and lover.
- gracious mom and mother-in-law.
- grateful daughter, sister, and friend.
- great coach.

I want to . . .

- know God.
- know where my vision fits into HIS VISION.
- wake up with purpose.
- create ways to have fun.
- be still.
- be full of vitality and life.
- be grateful and generous.

Whew! That is a lot more than you probably wanted to know about me. I want a lot. I want MORE.

Jesus asked him, "What do you want me to do for you?"

"Lord," he said, "I want to see!" **Luke 18:41**

What do YOU want? My guess is that you have been reading this book because something in you also wants MORE.

Yet I hear you ask, *What does it matter what I want?* Sometimes you just HAVE TO . . .

- pay the bills.
- get the kids through college.
- please the boss.
- make somebody happy.

I get it! Sometimes those are true necessities in our worlds. But I invite you to dig deeper than that. Look underneath the HAVE TOs and beyond the NEED TOs.

Come on, keep digging!

What do **you** WANT?

It is your genuine WANTS that reside closest to the core of who you really are! Your WANTS begin to speak to those values and relationships that matter most to you. They help you identify what brings great fulfillment to your heart.

Fredrick Buechner, a pastor, author, and theologian, once told a graduating class:

> The voice we should listen to the most as we choose a vocation
> is the voice that we might think we should listen to least,
> and that is the voice of our own gladness.
> What can we do that makes us the gladdest?
> What can we do that leaves us with the strongest sense
> of sailing true north?

— Frederick Buechner, *Wishful Thinking: A Theological ABC*[22]

If it is a thing that makes us truly glad, then it is a good thing that resonates deeply with the way God made us. It is our thing.

Have you ever thought about the fact that you—being you and finding joy in what you are doing—is actually bringing honor to the God who created you?

"What do you want?" is an invitation to know what makes you happy. Not only for the sake of your happiness, but for the sake of you living out your God-given S.H.A.P.E. to make your kind of difference in your world.

Imagine how your confidence will change in your future with each step you take toward knowing and embracing what you want.

> You know who you are!
>
> You know what you want!
>
> You know why you want it!

The possibilities for your future will continually expand, shift, and grow as your confidence changes. After all the hard work you have done to get here, this absolutely feels like a step in the right direction.

So . . . what do YOU want?

> *If you can't describe what you want,*
>
> *don't say you never had a chance.*
>
> — Dan Miller

Take some time to ponder the I WANT exercise in the workbook. Invite the Lord to give insight as you dig deep to find your own answers. This exercise is designed to help you be aware of what makes your heart GLAD and start to brainstorm a little about the WANTS that you have.

BUDDY CHECK-IN:

Check on your girlfriend here. Share what makes your heart glad!

Chapter 25
Taking Lessons from Moses

I AM OFTEN inspired, challenged, and moved by the story of Moses. There are some significant ways that his life claps together: from his being found in the bulrushes by the Pharaoh's daughter who spared his life, to returning to the Pharaoh years later to ask him to *"let my people go"* (referring to the children of Israel).

But in between those two moments are some significant times when Moses doesn't have to *remember* God. God actually shows up and invites Moses to meet with him.

- In a conversation in a burning bush (Exodus 3)
- In a tent of meeting (Ex 33)
- In the cleft of a rock (Ex 33)
- On Mount Sinai (Ex 34)
- In a cloud (Ex 34)

Each of his meetings with God were PIVOT moments for Moses — turning his thoughts and attention from the circumstances he was living in to the opportunities God was inviting him to.

When was a time you sensed God was inviting you to meet him? I encourage you to spend some time thinking about this. See what you can remember about that moment. If you can't recall such a time, that's ok. I encourage you to ask the Lord to bring those times to mind, or give you eyes to see or ears to hear his invitation now. I can promise you, he is close by, and he wants you to know him and to know his presence.

Several times, scripture shows us how the Lord built a beautiful relationship with Moses.

> "I will personally go with you, Moses." **Exodus 33:14**

> "I look favorably on you, and I know you by name." **Ex 33: 17**

In Exodus 34:6-7, the Lord told Moses his name, his real name.

> "Yahweh! The Lord! The God of compassion and mercy!

> I am slow to anger and filled with unfailing love and faithfulness.

> I lavish unfailing love to a thousand generations. I forgive iniquity, rebellion, and sin."

Then God said in Exodus 34, verse 10,

> "Behold, I am going to make a covenant. Before all your people **I will do wondrous works such as have not been created or produced in all the earth** nor among any of the nations; and all the people among whom you live shall see the workings of the Lord, **for it is a fearful and awesome thing that I am going to do with you."**

Wow!

Verse 28 tells us Moses was there with the Lord forty days and forty nights. In all that time he ate no bread and drank no water. And he wrote on the tablets the words of the covenant, what we know as the Ten Commandments.

What Moses didn't realize was that when he came down from Mt. Sinai, his face was radiant because he had spoken with the Lord. The people around him were afraid to come near him, so Moses put on a veil.

> **Ex 34:34** But whenever Moses went in before the Lord to speak with him, he would take off the veil until he came out.

When he came out and he told the Israelites what he had been commanded [by God], **35** the Israelites would see the face of Moses, how his skin shone [with a unique radiance]. So Moses put the veil on his face again until he went in to speak with God.

Earlier we talked about how we *cover up* or *put on* something to conceal the scars, the broken places, or the things about us that don't *measure up*.

But imagine PUTTING ON the glow of being in the presence of God.

Think of that! To be in the presence of the Lord and be transformed so much so that your countenance glows because of it.

Now fast forward into the New Testament to 2 Corinthians 3 (NLT). This is a moment where the past catches up to the present of Paul's time.

Paul writes in verse 7:

The old way, with laws etched in stone (Moses' tablets), led to death, though it began with such glory that the people of Israel could not bear to look at Moses' face. For his face shone with the glory of God, even though the brightness was already fading away. **8** Shouldn't we expect far greater glory under the new way, now that the Holy Spirit is giving life? **9** If the old way, which brings condemnation, was glorious, how much more glorious is the new way, which makes us right with God!

Now listen to this starting in verse 12:

Since this *new way* gives us such confidence, we can be very bold.

(Read that sentence over a few times. Let those words sink in.)

> **13** We are not like Moses, who put a veil over his face so the people of Israel would not see the glory, even though it was destined to fade away. . .
>
> **16** But whenever someone turns to the Lord, the veil is taken away. **17** For the Lord is the Spirit, and wherever the Spirit of the Lord is, **there is freedom. 18** So all of us who have had that veil removed **can see and reflect the glory of the Lord.** And the Lord—who is the Spirit—makes us more and more like him as we are changed into his glorious image.

The veil, designed to hide something that made the people afraid (or perhaps revealed that Moses was losing his *glow),* is removed.

Hear the Lord as he invites us to take off the plastic smiles, the masks, and the burial clothes.

And PUT ON his glory.

Think of it! We are not only invited to see God, but we too can reflect his glory to the world. We are made more and more like him as we are changed into his glorious image.

We now can dress as if we are preparing for a banquet.

> We take special pains to cleanse ourselves.
>
> We 'put on' special attire.
>
> We can present ourselves with confidence before the host.

Our host, Jesus, has chosen to invite us to his banquet, to meet with him, to spend time with him as close friends. When we spend time with someone, we develop a closeness, *an intimacy.* As we spend more time with them, we begin to *take on their image.*

*We are **transformed.***

But our host has also provided the garment for us to put on! His glory!

The Passion Translation of verse 18 reads:

...with no veil we all become like mirrors who brightly reflect the glory of the Lord Jesus. We are being transfigured into his very image as we move from one brighter level of glory to another. And this glorious transfiguration comes from the Lord, who is the Spirit.

We PUT ON the ever-increasing glory of the Lord!

Dear woman! **THIS is where our CONFIDENCE comes from!**

We can be confident women because we, being who we really are, who we were created to be, are reflecting the glory of the Lord Jesus, our very present, completely intimate Creator, Designer, Lord, and Savior.

Since this new way gives us such confidence, we can be very bold.

We have been CHOSEN to Know God and to be KNOWN by him.

Remember our formula:

Honesty + Remembering = Intimacy, which leads to confidence.

I invite you, for just a moment, to imagine that the room you sit in now is not just any room, but a banquet hall.

I would ask you to close your physical eyes, and use your imagination to lift your spiritual eyes to take in all the sights, sounds, and wonders of your new space.

You are standing at the door with your invitation in your hands.

How does it feel to be chosen to come into the presence of the King of Kings, Your Creator, Your Redeemer, the Spirit of the Living God?

Are you excited to see him? Are you thrilled to be here, elated to spend time with your host?

Or are you afraid?

> What will he think of me?
>
> What if I'm not good enough?
>
> What if _____ (fill in the blank with your answer.)

You are greeted as you enter, and invited to leave your STUFF at the door.

> To take off the fig leaves that cover your vulnerability.

> To leave outside the burial clothes that cover the scars and dead places of your heart.

> To take off the veil.

> And PUT ON his glory.

God has given you everything you need to PUT ON to come into his presence.

> His SON paid for your ticket to the banquet.

> His Spirit is going in with you—you are not alone.

How will you respond to this gracious invitation?

BUDDY CHECK-IN:

Talk with your girlfriend about what it feels like to have your invitation in your hand to come into the presence of your Creator. What does it look like to "PUT ON his glory"?

Chapter 26
Envisioning What's Possible?

Whatever the mind can conceive and believe, it can achieve.

— Napoleon Hill

HAVE YOU EVER taken the time to envision in detail how you would like your life to unfold? Not just think about it or even write things down. But allow yourself to see it—to taste it—to believe it.

Read Napoleon Hill's quote again.

"Whatever the mind can conceive and believe, the mind can achieve."[23]

It is one thing to conceive a plan or a direction for our future. But it is quite another to actually believe it is possible. Many times we are pretty good at thinking we believe something when we really don't.

The clearer you can become on what you want in your life—and truly believe it is possible—the easier it will be to do what you need to do to accomplish it.

This is yet another opportunity for you to PIVOT: to turn from the honest reflection of what is REAL in your life and pivot toward what is possible and achievable in your future.

This is where you pay close attention to what God is inviting you to and listen for where you can use your influence to make your difference. New confidence comes from taking new steps forward.

Envisioning what's possible is much like the chrysalis of a butterfly (or preparation leading to the chrysalis), which includes . . .

- the hard work of owning what's real about who you really are and how you feel about that, much like the caterpillar does on the leaf.

- the hard work of asking the hard questions and listening to what your answers reveal about you and your stuck places, much like the early stages of the chrysalis.

- those times when so much is going on internally that nobody else sees, even though we feel like it must be obvious.

After all that comes a moment in the chrysalis, just before the butterfly emerges, when the changes she has been experiencing are slowly beginning to show.

For you, this is the point you begin to see the fruit of all the hard work you have done.

You feel the changes that are happening within you.

You swell with energy and confidence as you look at the possibilities.

You begin to breathe fresh air and feel the newness of life.

This is the moment where your chrysalis begins to break away and the butterfly emerges.

At first you feel quite fragile. Your wings are very soft and wrapped around you, much like a newborn baby would be swaddled in her blanket.

You are reborn—made new. You are learning to take your first steps all over again, especially if you are starting a new job or relationship, or a new phase of life. You have to learn to walk again by taking small baby steps at first.

You are excited, but it is a reserved excitement because you have never been in this new place before. You know that the potential is there, but there is a bit of fear in this step.

It will feel kind of scary, and like work when you first start doing this new thing. First steps are rarely taken with confidence. You take them carefully, cautiously, yet aware of the newness, all the while sensing the beauty and growth. You feel it.

But never having done this before, you proceed carefully, building confidence with each new step.

That's where the growth you have worked hard for begins to shine. Once again you must trust the process; trust you are continuing to grow; trust you are breaking through to something new, something greater, something more!

Something MORE!

As the chrysalis drops away, the butterfly begins to emerge.

You step into those possibilities with purpose, direction, and confidence.

What do you see ahead of you?

> *Hope or optimism is not about denying reality;*
> *it's about seeing the possibilities for creating a better reality*
> *than you currently have.*
> *Every problem brings with it the seed of a solution,*
> *and I believe that the search for a solution*
> *can itself be inspiring and hopeful.*
> *If you lose hope, you will not be looking for solutions*
> *and will miss them even if they pass right in front of your nose.*
> — Dan Miller, *Wisdom Meets Passion*[4]

Often, I have heard people say, *I would boldly take my next steps if I only knew what direction to go.* The assumption is that once they figure out that THING they are supposed to do, they will go do it. With confidence.

I know that throughout the book I have talked about making your difference or doing what God made you to do. I recognize that those comments may imply that there is ONE thing that we are made to do. We just need to figure out what that is.

At times we are able to see in great detail and vivid color where we want to go. Those are the times when we move boldly with oodles of confidence as we take our next steps. We KNOW where we are going. And we have some sense of how to get from point A to point B.

But often we can't see the details. We feel like we are driving in a fog. We must drive more slowly and pay extra attention so we don't miss the next turn. We may have traveled this road before, but in the fog, we become less confident.

We still must have some sense of our destination, but it might be like saying we are going to the mall instead of saying "T.J. Maxx." Our aim is still forward, just not as direct.

It is true, we need clarity before we take action; we do need that bullseye to aim for. Without it, we are unable to point ourselves in the right direction. When we take time to envision what we want at the end of our destination, we are much more likely to arrive at the place we want to be. The clearer we can get about our bullseye destination, the better off we are.

But when we can't see the specifics, we can still have a sense of direction based on the values, qualities, characteristics that we want to be true of us when we reach our destination. Even though we may not know exactly what role we will play or the position we will have, we can know a great deal about what we want it to look like.

The work you've done this far can help you paint a clearer picture. You don't need the whole picture painted, just enough to help you move forward.

If you go back through your workbook, you will discover a lot of truth about who you want to be. You may not have written it down exactly like that yet, but there are values, characteristics, and qualities that you want to manifest. Knowing what these are helps you to align your actions with those things that matter most to you. That way, when you reach your destination, you have arrived with the values that make a difference.

> *The truth is, you cannot have confidence*
> *if you're not congruent about what you're doing.*
> *Many people succeed at the wrong things, only to find*
>
> *that they've been pursuing the wrong goals.*
>
> — Dr. Ben Hardy

Before you sit down with your workbook, I have a couple of exercises I use to help clients gain clarity about their bullseye. I invite you to choose one of these and play it out. See what you can learn about who you want to be and where you want to end up.

Exercise 1:

It's your 80th birthday party (or your 60th wedding anniversary). There is a program which involves toasts made in your honor by the people that matter most to you. Who do you want to attend your party? Who would you want to make the speeches? What would you want them to be able to say about you?

Exercise 2:

Write your own obituary. You've seen them in the papers. Use one of them as a template if that helps you. What story do you want your obituary to tell?

I know for some, this can be quite intense to process. I understand. The first time I did this exercise for myself I was fifteen. I have since written an actual obituary for my daughter at the same age.

But considering what you want to be true of you at the end of your life—whether you die at fifteen or eighty-five—is very effective in helping you see if you are indeed living the life you want to be remembered for.

Based on what you learn about yourself, it is the time to take your next step in the right direction. You can't become clear on something without moving your life forward. You can't steer a parked car. Each step will affirm or deny whether you are on the right path. As you go, as you take action, you will gain more clarity.

BUDDY CHECK-IN:

Share with each other your insights on your birthday party or the obituary. What do you want to be true of you when others are looking back over your life?

Chapter 27
Let's Sum Up What We Know

A S YOU HAVE worked your way through the material in this book, you have already taken some pretty big first steps toward your future, which, if you have written it down, is now recorded in your workbook. It is my hope that as you walked through these pages, your understanding of who you are and your awareness of what you are good at will help you determine where you are going.

While it is not the purpose of this book to nail down your bullseye, I believe you have much of what you need to identify the characteristics you want to be true of you on the other side of your journey. Why not take advantage of all that work to begin to declare what you want your future to look like?

So... take a moment to reflect back on your insights from your study of you. Gather up your answers on the summary page of your workbook.

- What ***traits or characteristics*** jumped out at you as you worked through the S.H.A.P.E. section? What ***recurring themes*** continued to come up as you worked through your story?

- What ***values or qualities*** stood out that are most important to you?

- Review your ***I WANT*** section.
  - Which WANTS are aligned with your values?
  - Which WANTS need to be tweaked or eliminated?

- Review your *roles.*
    - What are the roles in your life that help you live the life you want?
    - What relationships are most important in each role?
    - What do you need to do to align your roles and relationships to your values?
    (Refer to insights you had at your 80th birthday party or the obituary.)

Now let's partner those insights with three more questions.

What Is God Inviting You To?

Your confidence grows as you learn to pursue and succeed at the things that matter most to you. You have made a list of some of those things in your workbook, but to be confident you are pursuing the right things, you need to allow yourself time and space for reflection, prayer, and meditation.

Not only does this allow you to be more connected with yourself, but it allows you to notice the *kairos* moments and to listen when God is speaking to you, pointing you to your best next step or your next connected relationship.

- At what point in your day will you set aside time to be still, to pay attention?

    It may be the same time every day or various times throughout the day.

    Your time may include prayer, scripture reading, or worship.

    It might include journaling, reading, or listening to music.

    But I invite you to set aside time each day—even if just for a few minutes.

- Consider how you will capture your *noticings.*

    You might write your insights in a beautiful journal you picked up on one of your travels, or you might prefer using a spiral notebook you pick up at a dollar store.

You might use your camera in your phone to take pictures of things that are meaningful. Or use the voice recorder to capture thoughts on the run. Or any combination of them all.

The point is noticing the invitation from God. The other part is capturing what we are noticing and seeing how these things line up with our design, our messages, and our influence in our world.

That adds confidence to what we are doing.

What Breaks Your Heart?

Many times when I am working with a client who has said *"I want to make a difference."* they also say *"I am passionate about . . ."* From there, they share something that they love to talk about, an issue they feel strongly about, or a problem they think they can help solve.

The word *passion* gets used often without fully understanding the original meaning of the word. The dictionary defines it as a *powerful emotion* such as love or anger, or *intense desire,* or *boundless enthusiasm.*

But the true meaning of the word is actually "to suffer." When we talk about the passion of Jesus, we are talking about his suffering, his pain, and his death. This is more than strong emotion or intense desire. Jesus suffered because of his great love for us.

> *For God SO loved the world, that he gave his only Son, that whosoever believeth in him should not perish, but have everlasting life.* **John 3:16**

That's passion!

In fact, when we say we are *passionate* about something, what we are really saying is we are **willing to suffer for what we love.**

Women who long to make a difference in their world do so by connecting with their *passion.* That means that they are willing to do the hard stuff, or give up more enjoyable activities, to focus their energy on something that really matters to them.

Often our *passions* are born out of our own pain, marked by the scars we discussed earlier. It is our desire that others don't need to suffer what we have suffered.

That is why you will see people who have experienced loss create an opportunity to raise awareness or support for those who also struggle a similar pain.

When my daughter died, I said many times, *If I have to hurt this bad, it better help someone else somewhere.* I wrote *Lovely Traces of Hope*[1] to share my story and help others who are grieving and those who are walking with a grieving friend or family member.

I host an online video chat called *Green Hope Gatherings* once a month to allow people who have experienced loss to have a safe place to share their pain, and also to encourage them to notice where they are seeing HOPE in the middle of the pain. My heart breaks for people grieving the loss of a loved one.

But this book is also a result of my *passion.* I have become very aware of the stuck places women find themselves in when they are ready to take some bold next steps forward. I know how hard it can be because I have been experiencing those things myself. My heart breaks for the woman who feels like she needs to get it together but can't figure out how.

That's why I'm a life coach. That's why I do what I do. I am willing to suffer for the sake of these issues, born out of my own pain—and my own victories.

- What are the areas where you are willing to suffer to make your difference? You have probably highlighted some of these as you looked at your own story and pain.

Now it doesn't mean that your service in this area needs to be painful. In fact, when we are contributing to the things that really matter to us, we experience a fulfillment that is beyond words. You might be hosting fabulous fundraising dinners for a cause, or helping to build a home from someone in need, or ____ (I'm sure you have an idea of some ways this plays out).

But it does mean that you are willing to do the hard work, go the extra mile, and use more energy to make those things happen.

Sure, my heart breaks for people as they express their stories of loss with me, especially parents who have also lost a child. But my work with those same people is also extremely rewarding as I share their burden and remind them that they are grieving, not "losing their minds," which is how it often feels because of the chaos of emotions they experience after loss.

My work with women like yourself is both inspiring and challenging. Every week I get to see women take courageous next steps in their effort to live truly authentic to who God made them to be. It is a thrill to behold those transformations. I am continually encouraged to do the same as I walk with them.

But there are times when it gets hard, times when I wouldn't do what I do if I wasn't passionately invested in helping others who are where I've been.

Take some time to reflect on your story.

What breaks your heart? What solution do you want to be part of?

Where Do You Influence Your World?

What difference do you make? I hope by this chapter in a book about how to get unstuck, you realize that there are many ways to leave your mark on your world.

I've shared this story earlier, but I want to remind you of it again. The day Leisha died, I was teasing that her impatience about getting her driver's permit was because she wanted power. You know, "behind the steering wheel, *vroom, vroom*" kind of power.

Some of her last words to me were "*I don't need power. I want to influence. I want to say, 'I'm going! Come with me!'*"

For me, her words have created one of the best definitions of influence I have ever heard. They have spurred me to keep going because you can't invite someone to come with you if you are stuck.

But as I ponder how we influence our world, I notice the importance of **reaching out in two different directions**. With one hand, we reach back to those who are just a little behind us in life or business. With the other hand we reach forward to those who are a little ahead of us.

To reach behind us means that we are using what we have learned in our journey to help others in theirs. We use our passions, skills, and abilities to support, mentor, coach, point, guide, and empower others to move forward with greater confidence.

> *Being a mess doesn't disqualify you from having an influence.*
> *You are designed to reflect the glory of God,*
> *and when you release the fullness of who you most deeply are,*
> *we will see God because we're finally seeing you.*
>
> — Emily Freeman

To reach forward means we willingly, intentionally learn from others. We find support that helps us take our own next steps.

Sometimes we become more focused on one direction over another. **If we just reach back**, we start giving—and giving and giving—until we have nothing left to give. Without building relationships that are building into us, we quickly become depleted and of little use to anyone.

But there is also a problem **if we just keep taking in**, always seeking the next training, joining the next program, finding the next "guru" that can give us the info we need to feel confident as we move forward. Don't get me wrong; we all need to keep learning. But just adding more information to our brains without applying that knowledge, or sharing it with others, the more "constipated" we become. Eventually, we again are of little use to anyone.

The value is in reaching both ways. Think about the effect that occurs when we reach back and reach forward at the same time. We are able to help while being helped. We are able to encourage someone else to grow and move forward, while we are growing and moving forward with the wisdom of those who have gone before.

That's powerful.

That's influence.

- Who are your **reach forward** people?

Perhaps your spouse, parents, teachers, mentors, coaches, special friends, or family members. From them, you have learned to live, to love; when to say no, when to say yes; when to dream and when to get to work.

I know sometimes we put our kids in the *reach back* column, but I can tell you I have learned a great deal from my girls. They are definitely in my reach forward group.

What have you learned from your reach forward people?

What can you do to tell them how much you appreciate them in your life?

- Who are the people in your **reach back**?

They may be co-workers, or new moms, or people in the community that need your skills, people that fall into your area of passion that we talked about earlier... We are all still learning ways we can influence our world.

For me, they may be friends, or people I coach or mentor, clients, or readers of my book. These have taught me much about the value of a story—theirs and mine. They have shown me what courage and confidence look like. They have challenged me to grow deeper, faster, so I can continue to say, *"I'm going; come with me!"*

What can you do to continue to build relationships with others who need you to be you in their lives?

Who are you influencing? How are you influencing?

I, for one, love the picture of community that comes from that kind of influence. Reaching out to those who are ahead of me, reaching back to those who are close behind.

That's the kind of difference I want to make. How about you?

BUDDY CHECK-IN:

Share with your girlfriend who some of the people are in your groups. By now, you will probably add one another to your lists. You have helped each other both reach forward and reach back and different times through this book. How will you say thank you?

Chapter 28
What's Next?

To each there comes in their lifetime a special moment
when they are figuratively tapped on the shoulder
and offered the chance to do a very special thing,
unique to them and fitted to their talents.
What a tragedy if that moment finds them unprepared or
unqualified for that which could have been their finest hour.

—Winston Churchill

BEFORE I LET my clients go, I ask them to create an action plan based on new insights and awarenesses they had in their session. I invite you to do that here as well.

At the end of each part in this book, I gave you a TAKEAWAY prompt to summarize your insights in each section. Between those pages and your workbook pages, you probably have a great many things you think you can or should do. And if that is the case, you most likely won't do anything with all that you learned about yourself through this book.

I invite you to look at your list of things and narrow down your action steps to the 1, 2, or 3 things that you most want to see accomplished in the next ninety days. If you try to tackle more, you may get nothing done. If you try to plan out a whole year of goals, most of the time you think you have lots of time to do it and end up not staying focused and seeing anything to completion. Again, nothing happens with all the work you have done.

Use these two questions to help you focus your next steps.

What Do You Want to Be True of You in the Next Ninety Days?

- What goal would make the biggest difference in your life if you could achieve it? (project complete, weight loss, book written (my personal goal))
- What needs to happen in order for you to succeed?

What's Your Plan?

- Break down your ninety-day goals into week-sized action steps and begin adding them to your calendar.

Now granted, before you are able to add what is most important to you in your calendar, you may first need to eliminate some of the stuff in your life that you clearly know you don't want. That may also spill over into your home and work environments and commitments. But just taking that step will ignite a boost of confidence, while at the same time making space for greater accomplishment.

And remember, as you begin to take those action steps, more clarity comes regarding your future. Your belief grows as you stretch your capacity to create the difference you long to make. That builds confidence.

As your confidence increases, your imagination for the future will expand, as will your ability to influence your world.

That, my friend, is what you wanted when you first picked up this book, right? Congratulations! You are there!

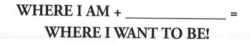

WHERE I AM + _____ **=**
WHERE I WANT TO BE!

— Paul B. Evans

TAKEAWAY:

Take a moment in your workbook to summarize those thoughts that stood out to you from PART SIX. This is an important follow up to all the hard work you have done through this process. Take advantage of the wealth of understanding you have gathered through these chapters.

BUDDY CHECK-IN:

You and your buddy have worked through a lot together. You have learned some remarkable things about yourself and one another How will you celebrate? Don't skimp on this step! You have done it!

Closing

The Power of Last Words

Be who God meant you to be and you will set the world on fire.

— St. Catherine of Siena

W HEN YOU ARE privileged to hear the last words of a person, whether he/she is just leaving your presence or at the end of their life, you learn to pay serious attention to those words.

Leisha's last words to me were of influence.

Mom, I want to influence.
I want to say to people, "I'm going. Come with me."

Jenn's Last Words

On June 7, 2017, my friend and mentor, Jenn Wenzke, lost her battle to the terrible ALS disease that threatened her body the entire time I knew her.

Our last conversation was at her home several weeks before her death. She was fragile but still had much to say. We spoke of her health, her family, and of course, the professional networking groups she had founded. I had benefited tremendously from them.

She said, "*You need to be coaching leaders.*" I knew she was exactly right.

We continued talking for a while, this time about my business and thoughts I had for my future. I spoke of interviewing other women in leadership and sharing their wisdom with the women in my *Green Hope Coaching* community.

Before I got the words out of my mouth, she was shaking her head—actually her whole little body in her great big chair.

"NO!" She insisted. "Be YOU! Your voice. Your message. NOW!"

My breath caught.

I knew this was not just any moment. This was THE moment. The moment that summed up all Jenn had been speaking into me since the first meeting two and a half years earlier.

Be YOU! Do what YOU do best! Do it NOW!

Her situation with ALS made it apparent that life was short. Don't waste a moment!

Her role as my mentor and champion had changed. She was now boldly launching me out to BE ME in the world!

My Last Words to You

My role is changing now too. I am no longer the author acting as your guide as you do the hard work toward transformation.

It is time, dear lady,

To own your value.

To use your voice.

To embrace your whole story and the lessons it has taught you.

To take advantage of the reach of your influence.

To make your difference

With confidence

NOW!

Jenn's last words are for all of us who want our lives to count. She modeled what it meant to live with confidence, even when she was afraid. To live authentically and confidently out of her design and her story. To use all that she was every chance she got.

When I couple Jenn's last words with those of my daughter Leisha's, I am convinced that I want to make a difference.

I want to influence. I want to say "I'm going; come with me."

I want to be an authentic, confident champion of women who grows a movement that empowers women to be their confident selves and champion others to do the same.

This is the **lasting legacy** that I invite you to be part of. Say this out loud with me.

> I am confident. I know where I am going.
>
> I am confident. I understand I am enough.
>
> I am confident. I realize my *ordinary* is extraordinary in the lives of others.
>
> I am confident. I hear the Spirit of the Living God
>
> > and follow his promptings today and every day.

Blessings on you, dear woman,

EnVision YOU: Unstuck and Confident

Be You! Make Your Difference! Now!

Resources and References

1. Burrus, Kathy. Lovely Traces of Hope. © 2016 by Kathy Burrus

2. Dillow, Linda. Calm My Anxious Heart: A Woman's Guide to Finding Contentment. © 1998 (NavPress, Colorado Springs, CO)

3. Cushatt, Michele. I Am: A 60-Day Journey to Knowing Who You Are Because of Who He Is. © 2017 by Michele Cushatt (Zondervan, Grand Rapids, MI)

4. Miller, Dan and Jared Angaza. Wisdom meets Passion: When Generations Collide and Collaborate. © 2012 48 Days LLC, (Thomas Nelson, Nashville, TN)

5. Warren, Rick. Purpose Driven Life: What On Earth Am I Here For?. © 2002, 2011, 2012 by Rick Warren (Zondervan, Grand Rapids, MI)

6. Gerth, Holley. You're Already Amazing: Embracing Who You Are, Becoming All God Created You to Be. © 2012 by Holley Gerth (Baker Publishing Group, Grand Rapids, MI)

7. Rath, Tom. Strengths Finder 2.0. © Gallup, Inc (Gallup Press, New York, NY)

8. DISC Profile:
   For a free assessment check out
   https://www.123test.com/disc-personality-test/

9. MBTI: Myers Briggs Temperament Inventory or the Jung Personality Test
   For a free assessment check out
   https://www.123test.com/jung-personality-test/

10. Harling, Becky. Rewriting Your Emotional Script: Erase Old Messages, Embrace New Attitudes. © 2008 by Becky Harling (NavPress, Colorado Spring, CO)

11. Life Story-Community: Discovering Who We Are Together. (Dallas Theological Seminar, Center for Christian Leadership, Dallas, TX)

12. Breen, Mike. Kairos, Continuous Breakthrough. © 2009 by Mike Breen (3 Dimension Ministries, Pawley's Island, SC)

13. Breen, Mike and Steve Cockram. Building a Discipling Culture. © 2016 by Mike Breen (3 Dimension Ministries, Pawley's Island, SC)

14. Shaw, Lucy, contributing author. God With Us: Rediscovering the Meaning of Christmas. © 2007 by Greg Pennoyer (Paraclete Press, Brewster, MA)

15. Kent, Carol. He Holds My Hand: Experiencing God's Presence and Protection. © 2017, Tyndale Momentum, (Tyndale House Publishers, Inc. Carol Stream, Il.)

16. Sittser, Jerry. A Grace Disguised: How the Soul Grows Through Loss (Zondervan, Grand Rapids, MI 1995, 2004) www.zondervan.com,

17. Young, William P. The Shack: Where Tragedy Confronts Eternity. © 2007 by Wm. P Young (Windblown Media, Newbury Park, CA)

18. Dobson, James. Emotions: Can You Trust Them?: The Best-Selling Guide to Understanding and Managing Your Feelings of Anger, Guilt, Self-Awareness and Love. © 1975 by Gospel Light Publications (Revell, a division of Baker Publishing Group, Grand Rapids, MI)

19. Gresh, Dana. Cedarville University chapel message. How to Overcome the Lie I'm Not Good Enough. https://youtu.be/h67MVF4xhGA

20. Wells, Simon. The Time Machine (2002) PG-13 movie adaptation of H.G. Wells novel.

21. Benner, David. The Gift of Being Myself: The Sacred Call to Self- Discovery. © 2004 by David G. Benner, © 2015 Expanded Version (InterVarsity Press, Downers Grove, IL)

22. Buechner, Fredrick. Wishful Thinkng: A Theological ABC. © 1973 (Harper & Row, University of Michigan, MI)

23. Hill, Napoleon. Think and Grow Rich. © 2017 The Napoleon Hill Foundation, Orignial Edition Copyright 1937 by Napoleon Hill (Sound Wisdom, Shippensburg, PA)

Acknowledgements

As I REFLECT on all the people who helped to make this work possible, I am reminded that it is not just the people I mention below who helped to make this happen. It is every woman, every client, every friend who has dared to have the conversations, challenge the status quo, take the next best step. You continue to inspire me to take my own.

Thank you to each one of you.

But I do have a bunch I want to publicly thank here.

Rennie, everything I do costs you something too. Thank you for your faithful love and support to do the next thing. Thank you for the meals you have fixed and the laundry you have done to allow me space to write. I love you as the sky loves blue!

To my girls: You two (and your dear husbands) bring me such joy!

> **Caitlin,** for listening over and over, for asking the questions, for challenging the thoughts as I processed, not just content, but emotions and doubts too.

> **Brielle**, for challenging my clutter of thought and helping me see what I was saying in vivid color, for your encouragement to be me, and your ability to capture my "real" smile.

Pat Hixon, for believing in me from the first moment I shared the idea of a new book. You ask the questions I need to answer not just in this process but in life! Thank you, my friend!

Beth Moore, for lending me your gift for arranging words as I worked through different sections of the book from front to back.

Janice Rayl, for letting me walk with you in our journey—and talking through all of it. You have helped to give life to so much of what is written here.

Doug & Jenny, for continuing to believe in me and your affirmation of book & workbook together.

Beta readers, Pat, Beth, Janice, Hazel, Deb, Shioni, Cheryl, Debbie, Lydia, Kathy, Pam, and even my brother Steve: THANK YOU! For daring to read the first draft, for giving input and suggestions, for wrestling with your stuck places and letting me hear the struggle. You helped make this book more real, more practical.

To Priscilla, Michelle and the women of Open Door Bible Church in Port Washington, Wisconsin: your insights and responses to the material at retreat was a tremendous help to this work. Thank you for your encouragement and support while we were together.

Tribe Girlfriends: Renee, Pamela, Nicole, Danielle, Doris, Judy, Marie, and the rest of the tribe, Thank you for not giving up on me when yet again I came asking for input. Your questions, suggestions and insights were so helpful.

Jeff Goins: Five years ago, you challenged me to say that I am a writer. It is with great joy to bring my second book to our 2019 Tribewriter conference. Your transparency over these five years has spoken to the core of my journey more times than I can number. Thank you for being you!

To my SO NOW SISTERS and the legacy left to us by Jenn Wenzke: We will carry on! Different than we expected, but we will continue to be women helping women to reach their unique greatness. To Bob, Diana, and Ted, I miss her too!

To Chandler Bolt, Gary Williams, Lisa Zelenak, my buddy Hazel Dahl, and the Self-Publishing School Community: Thank you for your encouragement, inspiration and support. I have so enjoyed working with you to complete this project.

To Kim Carr and her team at On the Mark Editorial Services: You have been a delight to work with. Thank you for capturing the spirit of the book and helping me run with it.

Last, but not least, THANK YOU to the *EnVision YOU* Launch Team! Thank you for believing in yourself and in me, and for choosing to spread the word about the book and the difference it can make in the lives of others. I am so grateful for each one of you!

About the Author

Kathy Burrus serves several roles in life. She is a wife, mother, daughter, and friend. She is a leader of worship that lifts the chins of people to see the face of God. She is a lover of stories, and more importantly, of the people who live those stories. That is what drew her to be a life coach: to help people discover who they really are and live their lives with confidence.

Drawing from her experience as a life coach and former ministry involvement, Kathy shares a message of hope and healing to women that is authentically transparent. As an author, Kathy's first book tells of the *Lovely Traces of Hope* she discovered as she grieved the overwhelming loss of her youngest daughter. Kathy speaks openly and honestly of the real struggles women face as we seek to make our remarkable difference.

Kathy and her husband, Rennie, have been married for over forty years. They are the parents of three beautiful daughters; Caitlin and Jack, Brielle and Jason, and Leisha. Kathy and Rennie live in Columbus Grove, Ohio.

Kathy enjoys hosting tea parties with her grandmother's china, listening to music that matches her mood, and observing nature in some of her favorite spaces. Add to that some precious time with family and friends, and she is one happy lady.

To schedule Kathy for your women's event or conference, or to learn more about her offerings and how she can help you envision yourself unstuck and confident,

email kathy@kathyburrus.com

or visit www.kathyburrus.com.

Lovely Traces of Hope

By Kathy Burrus

It's just another story of a mom desperate for hope after losing her child! Or is it? The one person that spoke significantly into Kathy's grief was her departed daughter. Listen in as Leisha influences her mom to see the tiny slivers of hope—like wisps of a dandelion.

Days after the sudden death of her 15-year-old daughter, Leisha, Kathy Burrus found Chapter One of a book her daughter had begun to write. Overwhelmed with grief, Kathy asked many of the questions we ask ourselves in life's most painful moments:

- Why is this happening to me?
- Where are you God?
- How can I deal with this unexpected pain in my life?

It was Leisha's unfinished book that penetrated deep into the torn and broken heart of her mother. As Kathy wrote to finish Leisha's story, Leisha pointed her mom to see the lovely traces God revealed about himself in random and unexpected ways. The Living One who Died became alive in Kathy's life like never before.

Do you struggle to see goodness from the God who has allowed your journey to have heart-wrenching pain? Do you long to experience the hope that God promises you?

God is giving you Lovely Traces of Hope each day. In this book, Kathy reveals how she began to see them—and how you can too!

AVAILABLE Online in Kindle or Paperback via Amazon.

kathyburrus.com/lovely-traces

CPSIA information can be obtained
at www.ICGtesting.com
Printed in the USA
FFHW021201150919
54992763-60692FF